RESTORATION, SEPARATION, AND FINAL ORDER

Restoration, Judgment, Resurrection, and the Completion of the Restoration Order

MBRS Book 4 —Master-Level Advanced Studies

The Official Student Textbook

DR. YERAL E. OGANDO

RESTORATION, SEPARATION, AND FINAL ORDER

The Official Student Textbook for the Master of Biblical Restoration Studies (MBRS)

By

Dr. Yeral E. Ogando

Authored and published by

Dr. Yeral E. Ogando

Adopted for instructional use by

Yahuah Institute of Biblical Restoration, Inc.

As the core text for

The Master of Biblical Restoration Studies (MBRS) Program

Licensing Notice

Scripture quotations are taken exclusively from Dabar Yahuah Scriptures – www.yahuahbible.com.

This textbook is produced for academic, instructional, and theological training purposes within the MBRS program and affiliated courses.

"All instructional texts used by the MBRS Program are independently authored and published by Dr. Yeral E. Ogando. The Institute adopts these texts solely for instructional purposes and does not own, publish, or receive revenue from them."

ISBN: 978-1-946249-54-8

1. AUTHORIZATION & INSTITUTIONAL STATEMENT

This textbook, Foundations of Biblical Restoration, is authored and published by Dr. Yeral E. Ogando and is adopted and approved for instructional use by Yahuah Institute of Biblical Restoration, Inc. as the core instructional text for the Master of Biblical Restoration Studies (MBRS) program.

All doctrinal positions, terminology, instructional structures, and evaluative standards contained within this volume are governed exclusively by Dabar Yahuah Scriptures as preserved in the Scriptures recognized by the Institute: the inspired writings of the Tanakh (Old Testament), the preserved Apokryfos, and the Renewed Covenant (New Testament) writings.

This text operates within a closed canonical and theological framework for the academic cycle in which it is issued. No external denominational systems, philosophical methodologies, speculative Yada Yahuah (theology), or institutional traditions are permitted to govern interpretation, instruction, or assessment within the MBRS program.

This Student Edition is authorized for instructional use solely within the MBRS program.

Unauthorized reproduction, distribution, or use outside of Institute-approved instructional contexts is prohibited.

2. PREFACE & STATEMENT OF PURPOSE

Foundations of Biblical Restoration exists because Scripture itself demands restoration.

This textbook was not written to defend denominational systems, preserve inherited theology, or harmonize philosophical frameworks with Scripture. It was written to allow **Dabar Yahuah** to govern Yada Yahuah (theology) without competition.

Modern theology often begins with assumptions and searches Scripture for support. Restoration Yada Yahuah (theology) reverses that order. Scripture establishes authority, defines categories, diagnoses corruption, and reveals restoration according to divine intent rather than human tradition.

This book serves as the **single, integrated instructional text** for the Master of Biblical Restoration Studies (MBRS). It guides the student from Scriptural Witness through*, Yahuah: Restoration Guide,* the ***Origin of Evil:** Biblical Truths Hidden in Plain Sight,* the **Three Humanities™**: *The Division of Humanity in Yahuah's Plan* - Volume 1, and th*e **Three Humanities™**: The Restoration of the First Humanity in Yahuah's Plan*—culminating in independent thesis defense.

3. STATEMENT OF PURPOSE

The purpose of this textbook is to:

> Establish Scripture as the sole governing authority
>
> Restore biblical categories obscured by tradition and translation
>
> Define evil without attributing corruption to Yahuah
>
> Explain humanity through the **Three Humanities™** framework
>
> Present restoration as transformation, not repair
>
> Prepare students to defend **Restoration Yada Yahuah** (theology)

independently and accurately

This text is not devotional. It is not speculative. It is instructional, corrective, and authoritative.

4. PROGRAM LEARNING OUTCOMES
MASTER OF BIBLICAL RESTORATION STUDIES (MBRS)

Upon successful completion of the MBRS program, the student will be able to:

1.Demonstrate Covenantal Reasoning across the full body of Scripture, integrating the Tanakh (Old Testament), Apokryfos, and Renewed Covenant (New Testament) writings without contradiction.

2.Explain Scriptural authority as divinely originated, canonically bounded, and covenantal preserved.

3.Define evil, corruption, judgment, and restoration using Scriptural categories alone, without reliance on philosophical or denominational frameworks.

4.Articulate the Three Humanities™ framework (First, Second, Third Humanities and the Variant) using Scripture-governed anthropology and lineage Yada Yahuah (theology).

5.Distinguish between sin, corruption, and Creational alteration, explaining why restoration requires transformation rather than moral repair.

6.Apply covenant language discipline responsibly, demonstrating how words govern doctrine and prevent theological distortion.

7.Defend Restoration Yada Yahuah (theology) from creation to consummation as a unified, Scripture-consistent system.

8.Produce and defend a master-level thesis grounded exclusively in Scripture, demonstrating doctrinal clarity, canonical consistency, and methodological integrity.

5. HOW TO USE THIS TEXTBOOK

This textbook is designed for **structured, sequential use** within the MBRS program.

STUDENT RESPONSIBILITIES

- Read all assigned Scripture before engaging commentary or explanations.
- Follow the progression of weeks and months without skipping sections.
- Use only Institute-approved Scriptural sources when completing assignments.

- Adhere strictly to locked templates, prompts, and evaluation criteria.
- Demonstrate mastery through clarity, Scripture use, and disciplined reasoning.

INSTRUCTIONAL STRUCTURE

- Each Term builds upon previous authority and doctrine.
- Each Month introduces defined instructional goals.
- Each Week focuses on specific Scriptural concepts.
- Assessments measure integration and reasoning, not memorization.

This text is not designed for casual reading.
It is designed for **formation, correction, and qualification.**

Students who attempt to bypass structure, introduce external systems, or rely on speculation will not advance.

6. ACADEMIC & SCRIPTURAL INTEGRITY STATEMENT

Enrollment in the MBRS program constitutes agreement to the following standards:

- **Scripture governs all conclusions.**
- **Dabar Yahuah is the highest authority.**
- No denominational, philosophical, or speculative systems may override Scripture.
- All work must be original, truthful, and accurately cited.
- Plagiarism, doctrinal innovation, or misrepresentation of Scripture results in disqualification.
- Advancement is evaluative, not automatic.

This program values **clarity over creativity, submission over speculation, and truth over tradition.**

The goal is not affirmation, but formation.

Authorized Textual Resources and Access

The instructional texts and Scriptural resources referenced within the Master of Biblical Restoration Studies (MBRS) program are made available through designated platforms.

Primary reference texts and supporting source materials authored by Dr. Yeral E. Ogando are openly accessible at www.yahuahdabar.com. These materials may be read online by any visitor. Registration allows users to download PDF versions of the source texts. These materials are publicly available and are not restricted to enrolled students.

The Dabar Yahuah Scriptures, including the Tanakh (Old Testament), Apokryfos, and Renewed Covenant (New Testament) writings, are openly accessible for online reading at www.yahuahbible.com. These texts are provided as the authorized Scriptural reference for the MBRS program and are available to all readers.

For Scriptural study and term-level consultation, students are instructed to use the Dabar Yahuah Scriptures App, including its Strong Concordance tools for Hebrew and Greek reference. This tool is used for confirming word forms, meanings, and Scriptural usage in alignment with the Institute's instructional framework.

The Student Edition textbooks, however, are not publicly distributed through these websites. Student textbooks are provided through the Institute's instructional platform or authorized course distribution channels, with the exception of the Amazon print edition.

These access distinctions are intentional and form part of the Institute's instructional and evaluative framework.

Contents

TERM IV — RESTORATION, SEPARATION, AND FINAL ORDER
MASTER-LEVEL PROPER · CULMINATING INSTRUCTION
Graduate Completion · Qualification for Thesis Phase

ACADEMIC ORIENTATION — TERM IV · MONTH 1

Term IV marks the final instructional term of the Master-level program within the Yahuah Institute of Biblical Restoration, Inc. This term assumes full mastery of all prior coursework, including Associate-Level foundations (Term I), Bachelor-Level formation (Term II), and the advanced Master-level construct of The Three Humanities™ introduced in Term III.

This term functions as a culmination of instruction, not as a research or thesis phase. No foundational material is revisited. Students are expected to reason with full covenant coherence, Creational precision, and strict methodological fidelity. All categories of creation, corruption, judgment, and humanity must already be clearly understood.

Term IV completes the instructional phase of the Master program by addressing restoration, separation, renewal, and final outcomes as revealed in Scripture. Its purpose is to confirm readiness for independent research and synthesis, not to conduct that research.

At this stage, students must demonstrate:

- Full command of restored Yada' Yahuah methodology
- Ability to integrate creation, corruption, judgment, and restoration into a unified Scriptural framework
- Precision in handling Creational categories without moral or emotional reductionism
- Consistency in Scriptural reasoning without instructional scaffolding
- Interpretive tolerance is at its lowest point in the program. Inconsistency, category confusion, or methodological drift indicates insufficient readiness to proceed beyond instructional study.

Successful completion of Term IV qualifies the student to enter the Thesis phase, where independent research, synthesis, and defense are required without further instructional guidance.

TERM IV - MONTH 1
TERM IV OVERVIEW
The Three Humanities™ — The Third Humanity & Yahuah's Restoration (Transformation, Renewal, and Final Purpose)

TERM IV is the final and highest stage of the Three Humanities™ framework. Where Term III diagnosed creation, purity, and corruption, Term IV reveals restoration.

This term answers the final question of Scripture:

What does Yahuah do with corrupted humanity, and what kind of humanity emerges from His plan of restoration?

TERM IV introduces The Third Humanity (PM + NW = MH) —not a return to Eden, not a repair of the Second Humanity, but a new humanity brought forth through restoration, transformation, and covenant fulfillment.

This term also reveals Yahuah's Restoration as:

- intentional, not reactive
- progressive, not instant
- transformative, not cosmetic

By the end of TERM IV, the student will understand:

- Why the Second Humanity cannot be repaired
- How the Third Humanity is formed, not evolved
- Why restoration is spiritual before it is physical
- How covenant, Spirit, and obedience define renewed humanity
- How Yahuah completes what He began in creation

TERM IV completes the Yada Yahuah arc of the entire Institute.

TERM IV STRUCTURE

Month 1 — The Third Humanity (PM + NW = MH): Introduction & Necessity

Month 2 — The Formation of the Third Humanity (PM + NW = MH)

Month 3 — The Identity, Walk, and Authority of the Third Humanity (PM + NW = MH)

Month 4 — Yahuah's Restoration: Completion & Consummation

THE THIRD HUMANITY — NECESSITY & INTRODUCTION

MODULE OVERVIEW

Why a Third Humanity Is Required

THE THIRD HUMANITY (PM + NW = MH)

Pure Men + Nephilim Women = Mixed Humanity (Partial Corruption)

Month 1 establishes why restoration requires a Third Humanity at all. Scripture does not present redemption as a patch applied to corrupted humanity. Instead, it reveals the necessity of a new humanity brought forth through covenant, Spirit, and transformation.

This month corrects the common Yada Yahuah error that assumes:

the Second Humanity can be morally repaired

corruption can be reversed through effort

restoration means returning to Adam

Scripture teaches otherwise.

By the end of this month, the student will understand that:

The First Humanity (Y+A=FH) was pure but vulnerable

The Second Humanity (AW + HW = N & NM + PW = N) is corrupted and enslaved

The Third Humanity (PM + NW = MH) is renewed and transformed

Restoration is not reversal, but fulfillment

Yahuah's plan always pointed forward, not backward

CHAPTER COVERAGE

- Demonstrate why restoration requires a Third Humanity rather than repair of the Second
- Distinguish restoration as transformation vs return/reversal
- Explain "born from above" as Spirit-origin identity using Exodus and New Covenant texts
- Show covenant fulfillment without replacement Yada Yahuah

- Trace the forward progression: Eden → covenant history → Messiah → new creation

The Three Humanities™ — The Third Humanity (Foundational Concepts)
- Chapter 1 — Why Restoration Requires a New Humanity
- Chapter 2 — Not Return, but Transformation
- Chapter 3 — Born from Above, Not Reformed from Below
- Chapter 4 — Covenant Fulfillment, Not Covenant Replacement

TERM IV · MONTH 1 — WEEK 49
WHY RESTORATION REQUIRES A NEW HUMANITY
Repair Is Not Enough

PURPOSE OF WEEK 49

This week trains the student to interpret why restoration in Scripture requires a new humanity rather than the repair of an existing one.

Students are taught to identify the point at which correction, instruction, and restraint are no longer sufficient, and why Yahuah introduces transformation at the level of being.

By engaging Book 4, Chapters 1–2, students learn to read the transition from judgment to restoration through Yada Yahuah, recognizing that redemption advances not by fixing corruption, but by calling forth a different humanity under covenant.

This week marks the interpretive shift from containment of corruption to initiation of restoration.

READ AND INSTRUCTION

- Yirmeyahu (Jeremiah) 17:9
  Corruption of the heart is internal and self-sustaining.
- Rómĕos (Romans) 8:7–8
  The fleshly mind lacks the capacity to submit to Elohiym.
- 2 Corinthians 5:17
  Restoration is defined as new creation, not reform.

Student Textbook Reading

The Three Humanities — The Rise of The Third Humanity (Book 4)

- Chapter 1 — The Third Humanity — and the Redemption of Yahuah
- Chapter 2 — The Call of Abram — Yahuah Chooses One Man Out of the Confusion of the Nations

Students must read both chapters fully before analysis.

Teaching Explanation

Restoration Is Triggered When Repair Fails

Scripture presents a clear interpretive boundary:

- The First Humanity (Y+A=FH) required preservation.
- The Second Humanity (AW + HW = N & NM + PW = N) required removal.

Week 49 trains students to recognize that neither preservation nor removal produces restoration.

Restoration begins only when Yahuah introduces a new mode of humanity rather than attempting to rehabilitate an existing one.

When Scripture stops correcting and starts calling, a new humanity is being formed.

Corruption Cannot Be Disciplined Into Alignment

The post-Flood world demonstrates that restraint does not equal renewal.

Law, memory, and survival remain, yet alignment does not self-generate.

This reveals a core Yada Yahuah principle:

Corruption is not a behavioral malfunction — it is a condition of inheritance.

The emergence of the Third Humanity (PM + NW = MH) - Pure Men + Nephilim Women = Mixed Humanity (Partial Corruption) reflects this reality: redeemable, yet unstable — capable of response, yet unable to self-correct.

Instruction can govern behavior; only calling can alter trajectory.

Calling Replaces Repair as the Method of Redemption

Abram's appearance signals a decisive shift in divine strategy.

Scripture does not portray Abram as corrected humanity, but as called humanity.

Separation precedes refinement. Covenant precedes transformation.

This reframes restoration through Yada Yahuah as:

- Initiated by Yahuah
- Anchored in covenant
- Sustained by obedience, not origin

New creation begins with divine initiative, not human readiness.

Why a New Humanity Is Required

Week 49 trains students to see that restoration requires:

- A new allegiance
- A new inheritance path
- A new covenant identity

This prepares the ground for the emergence of the Third Humanity — the Variant (Y $\oplus$ HW = Y), where transformation begins not through correction of lineage, but through intervention by Yahuah Himself.

When Scripture introduces covenant calling, it is inaugurating transformation, not repair.

Alignment Focus — Chapters 1 & 2

From these chapters, students must extract and apply:

- Repair Is Insufficient for Inherited Corruption
- Calling as the Mechanism of Restoration
- Separation as the First Act of Renewal
- Covenant as the Engine of Transformation
- New Creation as Replacement, Not Improvement

Key Terms and Definitions (Week 49)

- Restoration

  Replacement of corrupted alignment through divine calling.
- Calling

  Yahuah's initiation of covenant identity.
- New Creation

  Transformation of nature rather than correction of behavior.
- Yada Yahuah

  The covenantal act of knowing Yahuah through His self-revelation, instruction, and lived obedience. It is not speculative reasoning about Elohiym, but relational knowing grounded in faithfulness, encounter, and submission to His Word.

COVENANTAL STUDY TASK

Pause and complete the following:

- **Explain why corrupted humanity cannot be repaired through law or discipline**
- **Demonstrate how Abram represents initiation of new creation rather than moral reform**
- **Identify the interpretive signals that indicate Scripture is transitioning to a new humanity**
- **Show how covenant replaces correction as the driver of redemption**
- **Use Scripture and assigned chapters directly.**

Avoid psychological, moralistic, or modern restorative assumptions.

FINAL THOUGHTS ON WEEK 49

Repair maintains structure.

Calling initiates transformation.

Restoration begins where correction ends.

QUOTE REFLECTION

"Yahuah does not repair corruption—He calls forth new creation."

TERM IV· MONTH 1 — WEEK 50
NOT RETURN, BUT TRANSFORMATION
Forward, Not Backward

PURPOSE OF WEEK 50

This week trains the student to correctly interpret restoration within the plan of redemption by rejecting regression models and recognizing transformation as forward completion.

Scripture does not restore humanity by returning it to Edenic innocence. It advances humanity toward permanence through covenant, pressure, exile, and transformation within corrupted environments.

Using Book 4, Chapters 3–4, students are trained to identify how Yahuah advances the plan of salvation through mixed humanity rather than by isolating purity or repairing corruption.

Week 50 establishes that redemption matures under opposition and that covenant identity is forged, not preserved, by conflict.

READ AND INSTRUCTION

- 1 Corinthians 15:46–49

  The natural precedes the spiritual; completion follows origin.

- Hebrews 8:6

  A superior covenant replaces earlier structures without negating them.

- Revelation 21:1–5

  Restoration culminates in new creation, not restored origin.

Student Textbook Reading

The Three Humanities: The Rise of the Third Humanity — Book 4

- Chapter 3: From Yitschâq to the Formation of Yasharal
- Chapter 4: Into Egypt — The Covenant Family in the Lion's Den

Students must read both chapters fully before analysis.

Teaching Explanation

Restoration Moves Forward, Not Backward

Scripture establishes a directional rule within Yada Yahuah:

Origin does not equal Fulfillment.

Eden represents untested origin.

Restoration represents identity proven under pressure.

The Third Humanity does not recreate the First Humanity. It advances toward its restoration through covenant history.

Humanity Equation Reference:

The First Humanity — *(Y + A = FH)*

Yahuah → Adam = Spirit-first origin

This state is not revisited. It is surpassed.

The Third Humanity Is Formed Under Pressure, Not Isolation

Chapters 3–4 demonstrate that covenant identity does not survive by avoidance of corruption but by endurance within it.

Yitschâq, Yaăqôb, and Yoseph do not mature in protected environments but under:

- internal betrayal
- exile
- famine
- deception
- imperial oppression

This confirms the governing interpretive rule:

Purity preserved in isolation does not produce permanence.

Humanity Equation Reference:

The Third Humanity — (PM + NW = MH)

Pure Men + Nephilim Women = Mixed Humanity

The Third Humanity is redeemable but unstable, requiring transformation rather than repair.

Covenant Identity Is Forged Through Conflict

The formation of Yasharal demonstrates that covenant advancement requires:

- rivalry (Yaăqôb / Êśâw)
- exile (Haran, Egypt)
- family fracture (sons of Yaăqôb)
- betrayal (Yoseph)
- immersion in corrupted systems (Egypt)

These are not failures of the plan. They are instruments of formation.

Redemption advances by pressure refining alignment.

Egypt Reveals the Direction of Redemption

Chapter 4 establishes Egypt as interpretive proof that restoration does not retreat from corruption but confronts it.

Yahuah sends His covenant family into a Nephilim-shaped empire to:

- multiply
- expose false gods
- judge corrupted systems
- reveal His Name
- prepare deliverance

This confirms a core Yada Yahuah principle:

Redemption operates forward through corruption, not backward toward innocence.

The Goal Is Restoration, Not Repair

Repair assumes corruption can be fixed.

Transformation replaces allegiance, inheritance, and identity.

The Third Humanity does not return to the First Humanity by discipline or law.

It advances toward restoration through covenant fulfillment.

Humanity Restoration Equation Reference:

The Return to the First Humanity — (Y + RT = FH)

Yahusha (The Variant perfected) + Resurrection Transformation = First Humanity Restored

Restoration is achieved only at the conclusion, not by reversal.

Alignment Focus — Chapters 3 & 4
- From these chapters, students must apply:
- Directional Redemption (forward, not backward)
- Covenant Forged Under Pressure
- Mixed Humanity as the Arena of Transformation
- Corrupted Empires as Instruments, Not Obstacles
- Restoration as Completion, Not Repair

Key Terms and Definitions (Week 50)
- Transformation
  Change of nature and allegiance through covenant progression.
- Fulfillment
  Completion of origin through tested permanence.
- Progression
  Forward movement toward restoration, not reversal to innocence.

COVENANTAL STUDY TASK

Pause and complete the following:

- *Explain why restoration cannot mean returning to Eden*
- *Demonstrate how Yitschâq, Yaăqôb, and Yoseph advance covenant identity through pressure*
- *Identify how Egypt functions as a crucible rather than a deviation*
- *Show how transformation fulfills origin without repeating it*

Use Scripture and assigned chapters directly.
Avoid regression-based or repair-centered frameworks.

Final Thoughts on Week 50
Eden was origin.

YASHARAL IS FORMATION.

Restoration is completion.

Yahuah does not reverse corruption.

He overcomes it by finishing what He began.

QUOTE REFLECTION

"Yahuah restores by completing, not repeating."

BORN FROM ABOVE

Origin, Not Reform

PURPOSE OF WEEK 51

This week trains the student to correctly interpret origin language within the plan of salvation by rejecting reform, improvement, and continuity-based readings.

Scripture does not describe the emergence of the Third Humanity as moral recovery, covenant proximity, or behavioral correction. It presents new origin initiated by Yahuah Himself.

Using Book 4, Chapters 5–6, students are trained to identify how Yahuah establishes a people through birth procedures (blood, judgment, separation, passage), not through internal development within corrupted systems.

Week 51 establishes that redemption begins with Spirit-origin, not human adjustment, and that salvation requires a jurisdictional break before covenant identity can exist.

Read and Instruction

- Yochanan (John) 3:3–6
  Entry requires birth-from-above; flesh-origin cannot generate Spirit-origin life.
- Titus 3:5
  Renewal is regeneration by the Ruach, not works-based improvement.
- Ezekiel 36:26–27
  New heart and spirit are given prior to covenant obedience.

Student Textbook Reading

***The Three Humanities: The Rise of The Third Humanity*— Book 4**

- Chapter 5: From Slavery to Exodus
- Chapter 6: Signs, Spirits, and Judgment in Egypt

Instructional constraint: Chapters must be read as procedural texts, not narrative accounts. Students are analyzing how salvation is enacted, not what events occurred.

Teaching Explanation

Birth Is the Governing Interpretive Category

Scripture establishes a categorical rule within Yada Yahuah:

Reform does not equal Origin

Reform assumes continuity of nature.

Birth establishes discontinuity of origin.

When reading Chapters 5–6, the student must treat all deliverance language as origin-establishing, not corrective. This rule governs John 3 and controls how Exodus material is interpreted.

Humanity Equation Reference:

The Third Humanity — *(PM + NW = MH)*

Pure Men + Nephilim Women = Mixed Humanity

Mixed Humanity is redeemable but not self-originating. Any reading that assumes internal reform violates this category rule.

Corrupted Systems Cannot Generate Covenant Identity

Chapters 5–6 require students to distinguish between:

- Location and jurisdiction
- Proximity to covenant and possession of covenant life

Egypt functions as an interpretive control point: a fully developed system cannot produce covenant identity from within itself. Students must therefore read bondage, plagues, and separation as jurisdictional disengagement, not moral instruction.

Interpretive restriction:

Do not read Egypt as an environment to be improved.

Read it as a system whose claim must be terminated.

Divine Descent Precedes Human Movement

A governing sequence is established:

Yahuah descends → jurisdiction is asserted → separation becomes possible

Students are trained here to reject ascent-based readings (human effort reaching Elohiym). Chapters 5–6 establish that salvation begins with divine initiation, not human readiness.

This rule governs how the Third Humanity is brought into existence.

Humanity Equation Reference:

The Third Humanity — *(PM + NW = MH)*

Pure Men + Nephilim Women = Mixed Humanity

Judgment Is a Required Precondition for New Origin

Judgment in Chapters 5–6 must be read as procedural, not punitive.

The student must identify that judgment:

- terminates hostile claims
- exposes counterfeit authority
- clears jurisdiction for new identity

Any reading that treats judgment as excessive, symbolic, or secondary misunderstands its function within origin logic.

Judgment does not follow birth.

Judgment enables birth.

Blood Marks Legal Separation, Not Moral Achievement

Week 51 trains the student to identify blood as a boundary marker, not a merit indicator.

Blood signifies:

- transfer of ownership
- termination of prior claim
- eligibility for passage

This establishes the interpretive rule that salvation is marked, not earned. Students must not read blood imagery devotionally or metaphorically. It functions as a legal sign within covenant procedure.

Passage Establishes New Identity

Chapters 5–6 require the student to read movement not as escape but as transition of state.

The controlling pattern is:

old jurisdiction → terminated

new identity → constituted

This is the operative logic behind "born from above." Passage is not travel; it is reclassification.

Birth Serves the Larger Restoration Arc

Week 51 also trains students to hold the end-state in view without collapsing stages.

Humanity Equation References:

The First Humanity — *(Y + A = FH)*

Yahuah → Adam = Spirit-first origin

The Return to the First Humanity — *(Y + RT = FH)*

Yahuah + Resurrection Transformation = First Humanity Restored

The Third Humanity does not equal the First Humanity. Birth initiates the process that will only be completed at resurrection transformation.

ALIGNMENT FOCUS — CHAPTERS 5 & 6

- Birth vs Reform as a categorical distinction
- Corrupted systems as jurisdictional barriers, not training grounds
- Divine descent as the initiation of salvation
- Judgment as procedural necessity
- Blood as legal separation
- Passage as identity transition
- Birth as a stage within the full restoration arc

KEY TERMS AND DEFINITIONS (WEEK 51)

- Birth (Covenantal)

  Establishment of new origin by divine initiation.
- Jurisdiction

Authority determining ownership, allegiance, and identity.

- Separation
Termination of a prior claim enabling covenant transfer.

COVENANTAL STUDY TASK

Pause and complete the following:

- ***Identify where Chapters 5–6 prohibit reform-based readings***
- ***Demonstrate how "birth" functions as an origin category, not metaphor***
- ***Explain why judgment must precede new identity***
- ***Show how blood and passage operate as legal mechanisms***
- ***Apply the Humanity Equations to maintain stage clarity***

Use Scripture and assigned chapters directly.

Avoid devotional, moral, or improvement-centered frameworks.

FINAL THOUGHTS ON WEEK 51

The Third Humanity is not corrected into existence.

Humanity Equation Reference:

The Third Humanity — (PM + NW = MH)

It is brought into being through divine action that terminates one jurisdiction and establishes another. Birth, not reform, governs how salvation must be read.

QUOTE REFLECTION

"What is born cannot be repaired into existence."

TERM IV · MONTH 1 — WEEK 52
COVENANT FULFILLMENT
Restoration Without Replacement

PURPOSE OF WEEK 52

This week trains the student to correctly interpret covenant continuity within the plan of salvation by rejecting replacement-based readings and misinterpretations of failure.

Scripture does not present covenant as conditional on purity, success, or stability. It presents covenant as preserved, disciplined, and fulfilled across time, even when corruption within the people is exposed.

Using Book Four, Chapters 7–8, students are trained to identify how Yahuah sustains, disciplines, and advances a Third Humanity without discarding covenant, revealing restoration as fulfillment rather than cancellation or substitution.

READ AND INSTRUCTION

- Yirmeyahu (Jeremiah) 31:31–34
  Renewal internalizes covenant instruction; it does not abolish covenant structure.
- Mattityahu (Matthew) 5:17
  Fulfillment completes covenant purpose; it does not negate prior instruction.
- Rómĕos (Romans) 8:1–4
  Covenant requirement is fulfilled through transformed life, not external enforcement.

Student Textbook Reading

The Three Humanities: The Rise of The Third Humanity — Book 4
- Chapter 7: The Sea, the Calf, and the Third Humanity
- Chapter 8: The Forty Years in the Wilderness

Instructional constraint: Chapters must be read as covenantal case studies, not moral narratives. Students are evaluating how covenant responds to failure, not recounting events.

Teaching Explanation

Covenant Is Preserved Through Failure, Not Invalidated by It

Scripture establishes a governing interpretive rule within Yada Yahuah:

Failure does not equal Covenant Termination

When reading Chapters 7–8, the student must resist readings that treat rebellion, instability, or corruption as evidence that covenant has failed or been revoked.

The presence of judgment, discipline, and delay indicates covenant enforcement, not covenant abandonment.

Humanity Equation Reference:

The Third Humanity — *(PM + NW = MH)*

Pure Men + Nephilim Women = Mixed Humanity

Mixed Humanity is unstable by definition. Instability therefore cannot be used as a criterion for covenant replacement.

Deliverance Does Not Equal Completion

Week 52 trains the student to separate deliverance events from restoration completion.

Crossing the sea terminates Egypt's jurisdiction.

It does not complete internal transformation.

Students must read Chapters 7–8 with this distinction intact. Any reading that assumes salvation should eliminate struggle, rebellion, or discipline misidentifies the stage of the plan.

This preserves proper sequencing within the plan of salvation.

Divine Presence Increases When Instability Is Revealed

A critical interpretive control emerges in the wilderness material:

Exposure of corruption results in increased divine presence, not withdrawal.

Pillar, manna, water, preservation, and guidance must be read as covenantal reinforcement mechanisms, not rewards for obedience.

Students are trained here to reject transactional readings of covenant (obedience → presence). Presence precedes and sustains obedience.

Discipline Functions to Preserve Covenant Trajectory

Judgment episodes in Chapters 7–8 must be interpreted as trajectory-correcting, not eliminative.

The golden calf, wilderness rebellions, and serpentine judgment expose unresolved corruption, yet covenant continues forward. Discipline operates to prevent derailment, not to justify replacement.

Interpretive restriction:

Do not read judgment as evidence of rejection.

Read judgment as covenant containment.

The Wilderness Is a Preservation Zone, Not a Detour

Week 52 requires students to read the wilderness as an intentional covenant environment.

The wilderness does not delay fulfillment accidentally. It functions as a controlled space where a Third Humanity can be sustained despite internal instability and external spiritual hostility.

Humanity Equation Reference:

The Third Humanity — *(PM + NW = MH)*

Pure Men + Nephilim Women = Mixed Humanity

This stage exists because Mixed Humanity cannot yet bear completion without transformation.

Healing Comes Through Looking, Not Performing

The bronze śârâph episode trains a precise interpretive rule:

Healing is granted by alignment with Yahuah's provision, not by human correction.

Students must read this event as a procedural marker pointing forward to fulfillment, not as an isolated miracle or moral lesson.

Humanity Equation Reference:
The Third Humanity — The Variant *(Y ⊕ HW = Y)*
Yahuah (Ruach) + Human Woman (Miryam) = Yahusha
The lifted figure establishes the fulfillment pathway without replacing the covenant people.

Fulfillment Completes Covenant Without Substitution
Week 52 maintains the final interpretive boundary:
Covenant is not replaced by Messiah.
Covenant is fulfilled through Messiah.

Humanity Equation References:
The First Humanity — *(Y + A = FH)*
Yahuah → Adam = Spirit-first origin
The Return to the First Humanity — *(Y + RT = FH)*
Yahuah + Resurrection Transformation = First Humanity Restored
Students must retain stage integrity: fulfillment completes what covenant began; it does not erase prior stages or people.

ALIGNMENT FOCUS — CHAPTERS 7 & 8
- Failure does not nullify covenant
- Deliverance does not equal completion
- Increased presence follows exposed instability
- Discipline preserves covenant trajectory
- Wilderness functions as intentional preservation
- Healing through divine provision, not performance
- Fulfillment without replacement

KEY TERMS AND DEFINITIONS (WEEK 52)
- Covenant Fulfillment
  Completion of covenant purpose without cancellation or substitution.

- Preservation

Sustaining covenant identity through discipline and presence amid instability.

- Alignment

Gradual reordering under divine authority rather than instantaneous perfection.

COVENANTAL STUDY TASK

Pause and complete the following:

- **Identify where Chapters 7–8 prohibit replacement-based readings**
- **Demonstrate how covenant continuity is preserved despite rebellion**
- **Explain why wilderness discipline does not signal covenant failure**
- **Show how the bronze śârâph functions as a fulfillment marker, not a substitution**
- **Apply the Humanity Equations to maintain stage clarity**

Use Scripture and assigned chapters directly.

Avoid replacement theology and moral-performance frameworks.

FINAL THOUGHTS ON WEEK 52

Covenant does not fail because humanity is unstable.

Humanity Equation Reference:

The Third Humanity — (PM + NW = MH)

Yahuah fulfills covenant by preserving, disciplining, and transforming His people until completion is achieved.

QUOTE REFLECTION

"Fulfillment completes covenant; it does not replace it."

CORE REINFORCEMENT
Origin · Transformation · Fulfillment

FUNCTION OF CORE REINFORCEMENT
This reinforcement exists to lock interpretive posture for the entire month.
It ensures that students:
- Do not collapse stages
- Do not moralize covenant processes
- Do not introduce replacement logic
- Do not read outcomes into procedures prematurely

This module governs how all material in Weeks 49–52 must be read, regardless of narrative detail.

Master Interpretive Axis (Month-Level Control)
Origin → Transformation → Fulfillment
- These are non-interchangeable stages within Yada Yahuah.
- Origin establishes existence
- Transformation reshapes alignment
- Fulfillment completes covenant purpose

Any reading that merges these stages produces doctrinal distortion.

Humanity-State Control (Mandatory Reference)
All interpretation in Term IV · Month 1 must maintain stage clarity using the locked equations.

THE FIRST HUMANITY
(Y + A = FH)
Spirit-first origin
This state is not re-entered by history.

THE THIRD HUMANITY

(PM + NW = MH)

Mixed Humanity

This is the active covenant arena of this month.

Instability is assumed.

Failure is expected.

Preservation—not replacement—is the operative rule.

THE THIRD HUMANITY — THE VARIANT

(Y $\oplus$ HW = Y)

Transformation begins

This is the fulfillment mechanism, not covenant cancellation.

THE RETURN TO THE FIRST HUMANITY

(Y + RT = FH)

Final restoration

This is future, not wilderness-achieved.

MONTH-LEVEL INTERPRETIVE RULES (NON-NEGOTIABLE)

Rule 1: Deliverance does not equal Completion

Exodus events terminate hostile jurisdiction.

They do not complete restoration.

Students must never read deliverance as arrival.

Rule 2: Exposure of Corruption does not equal Covenant Failure

Rebellion, idolatry, and instability reveal the condition of the Third Humanity.

They do not invalidate covenant.

Judgment functions as containment, not rejection.

Rule 3: Presence Increases Where Instability Is Exposed

Within Term IV · Month 1:

- Divine presence intensifies

- Supervision increases
- Provision becomes constant

Presence is not reward-based.

It is preservation-based.

Rule 4: Wilderness Is Intentional, Not Accidental

The wilderness must always be read as:

- A controlled environment
- A preservation zone
- A transformation corridor

It is never a detour, delay, or punishment-only space.

Rule 5: Fulfillment Never Replaces Covenant

Messiah fulfills covenant functionally.

He does not replace:

- The people
- The covenant
- The process

Any reading that implies substitution violates the month's core logic.

Common Interpretive Errors This Core Prevents

Students must be trained to actively reject:

- Regression to Eden models
- Moral-improvement salvation frameworks
- Replacement Yada Yahuah
- Perfection-at-deliverance assumptions
- Event-centered readings divorced from covenant sequence

These are reading failures, not doctrinal disagreements.

Month-Level Outcome (What the Student Should Now Be Able to Do)

By the end of Term IV · Month 1, a student should be able to:

- Identify which stage of humanity a passage belongs to
- Apply the correct equation without explanation
- Distinguish procedure from outcome
- Read failure as data, not disqualification

Maintain covenant continuity without collapsing fulfillment forward

This is interpretive maturity, not belief attainment.

FINAL REINFORCEMENT STATEMENT

Term IV · Month 1 teaches one governing discipline:

Yahuah does not abandon covenant because humanity is unstable.

 He fulfills covenant by carrying instability forward until transformation is complete.

Stage clarity preserves truth.

TERM IV· MONTH 2
THE THIRD HUMANITY — FORMATION & PROCESS

MODULE OVERVIEW

How the Third Humanity Is Formed

Month 2 establishes how the Third Humanity is formed once its necessity has been proven.

Scripture does not present restoration as a legal adjustment, moral improvement, or institutional correction. Instead, it reveals formation as a divine, ordered process in which corruption is removed, old identity is terminated, new origin is introduced, and obedience emerges from internal alignment rather than external enforcement.

This month corrects the common Yada Yahuah errors that assume:

- forgiveness completes restoration
- obedience can be produced by law, leadership, or coercion
- regeneration can occur without the death of the old humanity
- systems, covenants, or lineage can generate new life

Scripture teaches otherwise.

By the end of this month, the student will understand that:

- The Third Humanity is formed, not reformed
- Redemption operates by removal and replacement, not coexistence
- Regeneration originates only through the Spirit of Yahuah
- The old humanity must fully die before the new can be born
- External systems reach exhaustion before internal renewal appears
- Obedience flows from restored nature, not imposed authority

CHAPTER COVERAGE

Month 2 trains the student to interpret salvation as process and progression, not event or status.

Using the assigned chapters, students will:

- Identify redemption as a two-part action (removal → replacement)
- Recognize regeneration as Spirit-origin, not leadership or heritage
- Trace the termination of the old humanity through prophets, empires, and silence
- Distinguish birth of new humanity from reform of old systems
- Establish obedience as law written on the heart, not external enforcement
- Understand formation as preparation for restoration, not restoration itself

The Three Humanities™ — The Rise of the Third Humanity – Book 4
(Process, Means, and Divine Action)
Term IV – Month 2 - Week 53
Book 4 — Chapters 9–10
- Giants (Nephilim), False Prophets, and the Rise of Yahusha Son of Nun
- Yahusha Son of Nun and the War Against the Nephilim Nations
Formation Focus:
Removal of what cannot inherit → replacement with faithful carriers

The Three Humanities™ — The Rise of the Third Humanity – Book 4
Term IV – Month 2 -Week 54
Book 4 — Chapters 11–12
- The Era of the Judges, the Rejection of Yahuah, and the Rise of the Kings
- The Rise of the Kings and the Establishment of the Covenant Throne
Formation Focus:
Leadership exposes origin failure → regeneration required

The Three Humanities™ — The Rise of the Third Humanity – Book 4
Term IV – Month 2 - Week 55
Book 4 — Chapters 13–14
- The Era of the Prophets, the Rise of Empires, and the Final Call of Malachi
- The Silence of Four Hundred Years and the World Prepared for the Messiah

Formation Focus:

Death of the old order → juridical closure before birth

The Three Humanities™ — Yahuah's Restoration – Book 4

Term IV – Month 2 - Week 56

Book 5 — Chapters 1–2

- The Empire of Iron — How the World-System of Nimrod Became the World of Rome
- Humanity by the Arrival of Yahusha Ha'Mashiyach

Formation Focus:

External systems exhausted → law written on the heart

STRUCTURAL CONTINUITY STATEMENT

Month 1 established why a Third Humanity is required.

Month 2 establishes how that humanity is formed.

Necessity → Process

Introduction → Formation

Calling → Preparation

Month 2 does not complete restoration.

It forms the humanity that will receive it.

TERM IV· MONTH 2 — WEEK 53
THE TWO-PART REDEMPTIVE PLAN OF YAHUAH
Removal and Replacement

PURPOSE OF WEEK 53

This week trains the student to correctly interpret removal and replacement as a governing procedural rule within the plan of salvation.

Scripture does not present redemption as permission for corruption to remain. It presents redemption as a two-part action: what is corrupted is removed, and what can inherit is raised and installed.

Using Book Four, Chapters 9–10, students are trained to identify how Yahuah advances covenant fulfillment by terminating irredeemable elements (generations, bloodlines, and strongholds) and installing obedient carriers of covenant purpose.

Week 53 establishes that forgiveness alone does not produce inheritance; inheritance requires replacement.

READ AND INSTRUCTION

- Yasha'yahu (Isaiah) 53:5–6
  Removal of transgression precedes healing.
- Rómĕos (Romans) 6:6–11
  The old humanity is put to death so new life may operate.
- Êber (Hebrews) 9:26
  Sin is removed, not managed or accommodated.

Student Textbook Reading
The Three Humanities: The Rise of The Third Humanity — Book Four
- Chapter 9: Giants (Nephilim), False Prophets, and the Rise of Yahusha Son of Nun
- Chapter 10: Yahusha Son of Nun and the War Against the Nephilim Nations

Instructional constraint: These chapters must be read as procedural demonstrations, not ethical arguments or historical narratives. The student is identifying how Yahuah advances redemption, not why conquest occurs.

Teaching Explanation

Removal Is a Covenant Requirement, Not a Punitive Reaction
Scripture establishes a procedural rule within Yada Yahuah:
Inheritance does not equal Forgiveness Alone
When reading Chapters 9–10, students must distinguish between deliverance and qualification to inherit. The wilderness generation is not rejected emotionally; it is removed procedurally because unbelief prevents inheritance.

Humanity Equation Reference:

The Third Humanity — *(PM + NW = MH)*
Pure Men + Nephilim Women = Mixed Humanity
Mixed Humanity is redeemable but unstable. Instability is tolerated temporarily; unbelief that refuses alignment is not.

Generational Removal Preserves Promise Without Altering It

Chapter 9 trains the student to read generational death as containment, not failure of covenant.
The promise remains unchanged.
The carriers are replaced.
Do not read the death of the wilderness generation as covenant collapse.
Read it as covenant protection.

Replacement Requires Prepared Carriers

Yahusha son of Nun must be read as a replacement instrument, not merely a successor.
Replacement does not introduce a new promise.
It installs a carrier capable of executing the existing one.
This preserves continuity while enabling advancement.
Humanity Equation Reference:
The Third Humanity — *(PM + NW = MH)*
Pure Men + Nephilim Women = Mixed Humanity

Replacement occurs within the Third Humanity, not outside it.

Corrupted Bloodlines Are Treated Differently Than Corrupted Individuals
Chapters 9–10 establish a critical interpretive boundary:
Irredeemable corruption is removed.
Redeemable individuals may align and live.
Students must not collapse this distinction. Nephilim bloodlines and their systems are treated as structural corruption, not moral failure. Removal here is restorative to creation, not punitive toward persons.
Interpretive restriction:
Do not read conquest as ethnic or moral judgment.
Read it as creational sanitation.

Warfare Functions as Removal, Not Expansion
Week 53 trains the student to read warfare as procedural cleansing, not territorial ambition.
The land cannot host covenant life while corrupted structures retain jurisdiction. Removal clears the environment so covenant life can operate without contamination.

This aligns with the two-part redemptive rule:
- Remove what corrupts
- Install what can sustain life

Replacement Is Progressive but Decisive
The long war demonstrates that replacement is not instantaneous. Yahuah removes in stages and installs gradually to maintain order and stability.
Interpretive rule:
Do not confuse gradual execution with incomplete intent.
Replacement is definitive even when process is extended.

Fulfillment Advances Without Altering the Plan
Week 53 reinforces that replacement does not revise covenant intent. It enables

covenant execution.

Humanity Equation References:
The First Humanity — *(Y + A = FH)*
Yahuah → Adam = Spirit-first origin
The Third Humanity — *(PM + NW = MH)*
Mixed Humanity in formation
The Return to the First Humanity — *(Y + RT = FH)*
Final restoration remains future
Removal and replacement operate inside the Third Humanity stage to preserve the trajectory toward final restoration.

Alignment Focus — Chapters 9 & 10
- Forgiveness does not equal inheritance
- Unbelief triggers removal, not promise revision
- Replacement installs capable carriers
- Structural corruption is eliminated, not rehabilitated
- Warfare functions as cleansing
- Replacement may be progressive but is decisive
- Covenant continuity is preserved throughout

KEY TERMS AND DEFINITIONS (WEEK 53)
- Removal
  Termination of corruption that cannot inherit covenant purpose.
- Replacement
  Installation of aligned carriers capable of sustaining covenant execution.
- Inheritance
  Covenant occupancy requiring alignment, not merely forgiveness.

COVENANTAL STUDY TASK

Pause and complete the following:

- *Identify where Chapters 9–10 require removal before advancement*
- *Demonstrate how the wilderness generation illustrates containment, not rejection*
- *Show how Yahusha son of Nun functions as replacement without altering covenant*
- *Distinguish between irredeemable structures and redeemable individuals*
- *Apply the Humanity Equations to maintain stage clarity*

Use Scripture and assigned chapters directly.

Avoid models that equate forgiveness with permission for corruption to remain.

FINAL THOUGHTS ON WEEK 53

Covenant does not advance by negotiation with corruption.

Humanity Equation Reference:

The Third Humanity — (PM + NW = MH)

What cannot inherit is removed.

What can inherit is raised.

This is restoration by design, not destruction.

QUOTE REFLECTION

"You cannot install life where corruption refuses removal."

TERM IV· MONTH 2 — WEEK 54
REGENERATION BY THE SPIRIT
Origin of New Humanity

PURPOSE OF WEEK 54

This week trains the student to correctly interpret Spirit-origin within the plan of salvation by rejecting lineage-based, leadership-based, and institution-based readings of renewal.

Scripture does not present judgeship, monarchy, territory, or covenant office as sources of new humanity. These structures function as containers, not generators. Regeneration originates only where the Spirit of Yahuah acts. Using Book Four, Chapters 11–12, students are trained to identify how repeated deliverance without regeneration produces instability, and how Spirit action—temporary or permanent—defines whether covenant life can be sustained.

READ AND INSTRUCTION

- Yochanan (John) 1:12–13
  New humanity is born of Elohiym, not bloodlines, fleshly will, or human authority.
- Titus 3:5
  Renewal occurs through regeneration by the Spirit, not reform or heritage.
- Rómĕos (Romans) 8:9–11
  Indwelling Spirit defines belonging, life, and identity.

Student Textbook Reading
The Three Humanities: The Rise of The Third Humanity — Book Four
- Chapter 11: The Era of the Judges, the Rejection of Yahuah, and the Rise of the Kings
- Chapter 12: The Rise of the Kings and the Establishment of the Covenant Throne

Instructional constraint: These chapters must be read as diagnostic texts, not leadership studies or moral biographies. The student is identifying origin sources, not evaluating character success.

Teaching Explanation

Possession Without Regeneration Produces Collapse

Scripture establishes a governing interpretive rule:

Inheritance does not equal Regeneration

Chapters 11–12 require the student to distinguish between occupying covenant space and originating covenant life. The post-Yahusha generation inherits land but not Spirit-origin identity. This distinction explains cyclical failure without invoking covenant abandonment.

Humanity Equation Reference:

The Third Humanity — *(PM + NW = MH)*

Pure Men + Nephilim Women = Mixed Humanity

Mixed Humanity can inherit territory and office without possessing new origin.

The Judges Reveal Temporary Spirit Action, Not New Origin

The judges must be read as Spirit-activated interventions, not regenerative events.

- The Spirit comes upon judges to deliver.
- The Spirit does not indwell the people to regenerate.

This explains repetition without advancement. Deliverance resolves crisis; regeneration replaces nature. Chapters 11–12 train the student to separate these functions.

Cyclical Failure Is Evidence of Origin Deficiency

The repeated cycle in Judges is not random disobedience. It is procedural evidence that origin has not changed.

Interpretive restriction:

Do not read repetition as stubbornness alone.

Read repetition as absence of Spirit-origin life.

This preserves the two-part redemptive logic introduced in Week 53: removal precedes replacement; deliverance alone is insufficient.

Kingship Exposes the Limits of Structural Authority

The transition to monarchy functions as a stress test for flesh-based authority.

Students must read Shaul as evidence that:

- Position without regeneration collapses.
- Authority without Spirit alignment destabilizes covenant execution.

Kingship does not solve the origin problem. It reveals it.

Dawid Demonstrates Alignment Without Completion

Dawid must be read neither as idealized perfection nor dismissed failure.

Interpretive rule:

- Dawid demonstrates Spirit alignment, not regenerated humanity.
- Alignment enables authority; it does not replace nature.

This explains both Dawid's victories and his moral fracture without collapsing covenant logic.

Humanity Equation Reference:

The Third Humanity — (PM + NW = MH)

Mixed Humanity remains the operative stage.

Temporary Spirit Empowerment Is Not Indwelling

The Spirit's interaction in Chapters 11–12 is selective, situational, and withdrawable.

Students must not confuse:

- Empowerment for task

with

- Indwelling for regeneration

This distinction preserves the necessity of a future Spirit-origin humanity.

Regeneration Requires a New Origin Mechanism

Week 54 trains the student to hold regeneration forward, not backward.

Humanity Equation Reference:

The Third Humanity — The Variant *(Y ▯ HW = Y)*

Yahuah (Ruach) + Human Woman (Miryam) = Yahusha

Chapters 11–12 prepare for this mechanism by demonstrating that:

- Judges cannot regenerate
- Kings cannot regenerate
- Lineage cannot regenerate

Only Spirit-origin birth can.

ALIGNMENT FOCUS — CHAPTERS 11 & 12

- Territory does not equal transformation
- Deliverance does not equal regeneration
- Temporary Spirit empowerment does not equal indwelling
- Structural authority exposes origin deficiency
- Alignment enables function without completing restoration
- Regeneration requires a new origin mechanism

KEY TERMS AND DEFINITIONS (WEEK 54)

- Regeneration
  Creation of new origin through direct Spirit action.
- Empowerment
  Temporary Spirit enablement for function without nature replacement.
- Indwelling
  Permanent Spirit presence establishing identity and life.

COVENANTAL STUDY TASK

Pause and complete the following:

- *Identify where Chapters 11–12 prohibit lineage-based regeneration readings*
- *Demonstrate how the judges illustrate Spirit action without origin change*
- *Explain why kingship fails to solve the regeneration problem*
- *Distinguish empowerment from indwelling using the assigned Scriptures*
- *Apply the Humanity Equations to preserve stage clarity*

Use Scripture and assigned chapters directly.

Avoid leadership, success, or heritage-based frameworks.

FINAL THOUGHTS ON WEEK 54

The Third Humanity cannot be regenerated by better leaders, stronger systems, or inherited authority.

Humanity Equation Reference:

The Third Humanity — (PM + NW = MH)

Origin changes only when the Spirit originates life.

QUOTE REFLECTION

"What is not born of the Spirit cannot live by the Spirit."

TERM IV· MONTH 2 — WEEK 55
DEATH OF THE OLD HUMANITY & BIRTH OF THE NEW
Transition of Identity

PURPOSE OF WEEK 55

This week trains the student to correctly interpret transition within the plan of salvation by identifying finality as a prerequisite for new origin.

Scripture does not present prophets, exile, empires, or silence as reform mechanisms. They function as termination procedures that exhaust the authority, legitimacy, and capacity of the old order so that a new humanity can be introduced.

Using Book Four, Chapters 13–14, students are trained to read judgment, displacement, and prophetic silence as death-of-system indicators, not pauses or setbacks. Birth follows only after the old humanity's jurisdiction is fully concluded.

READ AND INSTRUCTION

- Galatians 2:20

  Old life is terminated so new life may operate.
- Colossians 3:9–10

  The old self is put off completely; replacement is required.
- 2 Corinthians 5:17

  New creation language signals irreversible identity transition.

Student Textbook Reading

The Three Humanities: The Rise of The Third Humanity — Book Four

- Chapter 13: The Era of the Prophets, the Rise of Empires, and the Final Call of Malachi
- Chapter 14: The Silence of Four Hundred Years and the World Prepared for the Messiah

Instructional constraint: These chapters must be read as closure texts, not revival narratives. The student is identifying where and how the old order ends, not tracing improvement attempts.

Teaching Explanation

Prophetic Ministry Signals Termination, Not Repair

Scripture establishes a governing interpretive rule:

Exposure does not equal Restoration

In Chapters 13–14, prophetic activity must be read as covenant prosecution. Prophets do not stabilize the system; they announce its insufficiency and impending end. The increase of prophetic confrontation indicates systemic exhaustion.

Humanity Equation Reference:

The Second Humanity — *(AW + HW = N) & (NM + PW = N)*

Corruption originating from fallen powers cannot be corrected within history.

Empires Function as Instruments of Exhaustion

Babylon, Persia, Greece, and Rome must be read as terminal pressures applied to the old order. Each empire exposes a different limit—idolatry, legalism, philosophy, or power—demonstrating that no structure governed by the old humanity can sustain covenant life.

Interpretive restriction:

Do not read empires as reform opportunities.

Read them as jurisdictional stripping.

Exile Removes Authority Without Creating New Origin

Exile operates as displacement, not regeneration. Chapters 13–14 train the student to separate removal of privilege from creation of life. The covenant line is preserved, but origin remains unchanged.

Humanity Equation Reference:

The Third Humanity — *(PM + NW = MH)*

Mixed Humanity persists across exile without internal replacement.

Silence Marks Juridical Closure

The four hundred years of supposedly silence must be read as procedural finality. No prophets, no visions, and no intervention indicate that the old humanity's administrative cycle has ended.

Interpretive rule:

Silence is not absence.

Silence is termination.

This closure prevents hybrid solutions and prepares for a new origin event.

Death Precedes Birth as a Structural Law

Week 55 enforces a non-negotiable sequence:

Termination → Introduction

Any reading that places regeneration inside the prophetic era violates this sequence. Birth requires a concluded order.

Humanity Equation Reference:

The Third Humanity — The Variant ($Y \oplus HW = Y$)

New humanity enters history only after the old jurisdiction ends.

Messiah Introduces, Not Repairs

When Messiah arrives, He does not reform institutions, restore empires, or revive prophetic systems. He introduces new creation.

This confirms the interpretive boundary of Week 55:

Transition is not continuity.

Birth is not evolution.

Transition Preserves the Restoration Trajectory

Week 55 also requires stage integrity to be maintained:

- Old humanity ends
- New humanity begins
- Final restoration remains future

Humanity Equation References:

The First Humanity — (Y + A = FH)

Spirit-first origin (not re-entered historically)

The Return to the First Humanity — (Y + RT = FH)

Yahusha (The Variant perfected) + Resurrection Transformation = First Humanity Restored

Final restoration remains eschatological

Alignment Focus — Chapters 13 & 14

- Prophets prosecute; they do not repair
- Empires exhaust old authority
- Exile removes privilege, not nature
- Silence signals closure
- Death precedes birth
- Messiah introduces new origin
- Stage integrity must be preserved

KEY TERMS AND DEFINITIONS (WEEK 55)

- Termination
  The concluded authority of a corrupted order.
- Transition
  The boundary between ended jurisdiction and new origin.
- New Creation
  An introduced humanity with a distinct origin, not an improved form of the old.

COVENANTAL STUDY TASK

Pause and complete the following:

- *Identify where Chapters 13–14 require system termination before renewal*
- *Demonstrate how prophetic activity exposes finality, not reform*
- *Explain why silence functions as juridical closure*
- *Show why new humanity could only be introduced after this closure*
- *Apply the Humanity Equations to maintain stage clarity*

Use Scripture and assigned chapters directly.

Avoid coexistence or continuity-based models.

FINAL THOUGHTS ON WEEK 55

The old humanity is not healed into new life.

Humanity Equation Reference:

The Third Humanity — (PM + NW = MH)

It is brought to an end so that a new humanity may begin.

QUOTE REFLECTION

"Birth requires an ending."

TERM IV· MONTH 2 — WEEK 56
LAW WRITTEN ON THE HEART
Formation Toward Obedience

PURPOSE OF WEEK 56

This week trains the student to correctly interpret obedience within the plan of salvation by identifying internal alignment as its only valid source.

Scripture does not present obedience as the product of empire, priesthood, law, fear, or institutional control. These mechanisms expose failure precisely because they operate externally. Using Book Five, Chapters 1–2, students are trained to read the arrival of Yahusha as the moment when external systems reach total exhaustion and internal transformation becomes the only remaining solution.

READ AND INSTRUCTION

- Yirmeyahu (Jeremiah) 31:33
  Instruction is written on the heart, not enforced externally.
- Yechezqel (Ezekiel) 36:26–27
  A new heart and Spirit produce obedience from within.
- Rómĕos (Romans) 8:4
  Righteous requirement is fulfilled through transformed life, not coercion.

Student Textbook Reading

The Three Humanities: Yahuah's Restoration — Book Five
- Chapter 1: The Empire of Iron — How the World-System of Nimrod Became the World of Rome
- Chapter 2: Humanity by the Arrival of Yahusha Ha'Mashiyach

Instructional constraint: These chapters must be read as system-failure diagnostics, not political or religious history. The student is identifying why obedience cannot originate externally.

Teaching Explanation

Rome Represents the Peak of External Control

Scripture establishes a governing interpretive rule:

Maximum control does not equal Righteousness

Chapter 1 must be read as the completion point of the Second Humanity's operating logic. Rome synthesizes political power, law, religion, philosophy, economics, and coercion into a single global system. Obedience is demanded everywhere—yet righteousness is absent everywhere.

Humanity Equation Reference:

The Second Humanity — *(AW + HW = N) & (NM + PW = N)*

Corruption governed by fallen powers cannot produce internal alignment.

External Law Reveals the Obedience Deficit

Rome proves that law can regulate behavior but cannot transform desire. This distinction is critical. Chapters 1–2 train the student to identify compliance without alignment as the hallmark of the Second Humanity.

Interpretive restriction:

Do not read Roman order as moral success.

Read it as final exposure of external enforcement.

Religious Authority Fails for the Same Reason

Chapter 2 demonstrates that Temple authority, priesthood, and tradition fail for identical reasons as empire: they operate externally.

- Pharisees enforce obedience through tradition
- Sadducees enforce obedience through institutional control
- Hasmonean authority enforces obedience through bloodline and power

None produce transformed hearts.

Humanity Equation Reference:

The Third Humanity — *(PM + NW = MH)*

Mixed Humanity can perform obedience rituals without restored desire.

Obedience Cannot Be Legislated

This week requires the student to separate instruction from origin.

- Law instructs
- Spirit regenerates

Without regeneration, law becomes either hypocrisy or rebellion.

Messiah Arrives at Systemic Exhaustion

Yahusha does not arrive to improve Rome or reform the Temple. He arrives when both have demonstrated total inability to produce obedience.

Interpretive rule:

Messiah is not corrective to systems.

Messiah is replacement of origin.

Humanity Equation Reference:

The Third Humanity — The Variant $(Y \oplus HW = Y)$

Yahuah (Ruach) + Human Woman (Miryan) = Yahusha (New Spiritual Humanity)

This is the first mechanism capable of producing obedience from within.

Law Written on the Heart Defines Formation

Obedience in the Third Humanity is not enforced alignment but restored desire.

Chapters 1–2 must be read as proving the necessity of this mechanism.

Humanity Equation Reference:

The Return to the First Humanity — $(Y + RT = FH)$

Yahusha (The Variant perfected) + Resurrection Transformation = First Humanity Restored

Final obedience aligns with restored nature, not imposed regulation.

Formation Completes the Month 2 Trajectory

Month 2 concludes with a clear interpretive sequence:

- Removal (Week 53)
- Regeneration (Week 54)
- Termination of old order (Week 55)
- Internalized obedience (Week 56)

This preserves stage integrity without collapsing restoration into premature fulfillment.

Alignment Focus — Chapters 1 & 2
- Rome = peak external enforcement
- Law regulates behavior, not desire
- Religious authority mirrors imperial failure
- Compliance does not equal obedience
- Messiah replaces origin, not systems
- Obedience flows from regenerated heart
- Formation completes Third Humanity readiness

KEY TERMS AND DEFINITIONS (WEEK 56)
- Internalized Instruction
  Divine law embedded through regenerated desire.
- Obedience
  Alignment flowing naturally from restored nature.
- Formation
  Shaping of the Third Humanity toward purpose through internal renewal.

COVENANTAL STUDY TASK
Pause and complete the following:
- **Explain why Rome represents the failure of external obedience**
- **Identify how religious authority mirrors imperial control**
- **Demonstrate why law cannot produce righteousness**
- **Show how internal transformation resolves the obedience problem**
- **Apply the Humanity Equations to maintain stage clarity**

Use Scripture and assigned chapters directly.

Avoid models equating obedience with fear, hierarchy, or enforcement.

FINAL THOUGHTS ON WEEK 56

Empires command behavior.

Religion enforces conformity.

Only restored origin produces obedience.

Humanity Equation Reference:

The Third Humanity — The Variant $(Y \oplus HW = Y)$

QUOTE REFLECTION

"Yahuah restores obedience by restoring the heart."

CORE REINFORCEMENT
TERM IV · MONTH 2
The Formation of the Third Humanity
(Process, Means, and Divine Action)

GOVERNING AIM OF MONTH 2

Term IV · Month 2 trains the student to correctly interpret formation, not forgiveness, as the operative mechanism of redemption within Yada Yahuah. This month establishes that salvation advances through essential change (origin replacement), not through moral correction, institutional authority, or covenant proximity.

Month 1 explained why a Third Humanity is necessary.

Month 2 explains how that humanity is formed.

STRUCTURAL THESIS OF MONTH 2

Redemption operates by divine action, not human response.

The Third Humanity is not:

- reformed Second Humanity
- disciplined old humanity
- forgiven corruption
- improved obedience

It is created.

This month enforces the rule:

Forgiveness removes guilt.

Formation replaces nature.

HUMANITY STAGES

THE FIRST HUMANITY

Humanity Equation

(Y + A = FH)

Yahuah → Adam

Spirit-first, pure, incorruptible origin

- Lost
- Not repaired
- Only restored at the end

THE SECOND HUMANITY

Humanity Equations

1. $(AW + HW = N)$
2. $(NM + PW = N)$

Angels Watchers + Human Women = Nephilim

Nephilim Men + Pure Women = Nephilim

- Corrupted beyond repair
- Produces empires, false religion, coercive obedience
- Must be judged and terminated

THE THIRD HUMANITY

Humanity Equation

$(PM + NW = MH)$

Pure Men + Nephilim Women = Mixed Humanity

- Redeemable but unstable
- Cannot regenerate itself
- Requires removal, death, and replacement

THE THIRD HUMANITY — THE VARIANT

Humanity Restoration Equation

$(Y \oplus HW = Y)$

Yahuah (Ruach) + Human Woman (Miryam)

= Yahusha

- New origin mechanism introduced
- Spirit-first humanity re-enters history
- Enables regeneration and obedience

THE RETURN TO THE FIRST HUMANITY

Final Humanity Equation

(Y + RT = FH)

Yahusha + Resurrection Transformation

= First Humanity Restored (Final State)

MONTHLY PROGRESSION LOGIC

Week 53 — Removal and Replacement

Key Reinforcement

- Forgiveness alone stagnates
- What cannot inherit must be removed
- Replacement follows death

Corruption is not managed.

It is eliminated.

Week 54 — Regeneration by the Spirit

Key Reinforcement

- Judges and kings expose origin failure
- Temporary Spirit empowerment does not equal regeneration
- New humanity requires Spirit-origin

Leadership cannot regenerate humanity.

Week 55 — Death of the Old Humanity

Key Reinforcement

- Prophets prosecute, not repair
- Empires exhaust old authority
- Silence equals juridical closure

Birth requires finality.

Week 56 — Law Written on the Heart

Key Reinforcement

- Rome proves external obedience fails
- Religion mirrors empire's failure
- Obedience flows only from restored desire

Obedience is not enforced.

It is generated.

Core Interpretive Controls (Month 2)

- Students must retain these controls at all times:
- External systems cannot produce righteousness
- Law instructs; Spirit regenerates
- Death precedes birth
- Removal precedes replacement
- Obedience follows nature, not pressure
- Messiah introduces new origin, not reform
- Restoration is future; formation is present

Diagnostic Summary

Mechanism	Result
Empire	Compliance
Religion	Hypocrisy
Law	Exposure
Leadership	Failure
Spirit-Origin	Obedience
New Creation	Alignment

Final Reinforcement Statement

Term IV · Month 2 establishes the irreversible logic of salvation:

Humanity is not healed forward.

It is replaced upward.

The Third Humanity is not trained into obedience.

It is formed into alignment.

This month closes with the Third Humanity ready,
but not yet restored.
Restoration belongs to resurrection.

MONTH 2 PAPER — TERM IV
Master-Level Assessment
Length: 3,000–3,500 words
Prompt
Explain how the Third Humanity is formed. Describe the two-part redemptive plan, regeneration by the Spirit, the death of the old humanity, the birth of the new humanity, and the internalization of divine instruction. Support your argument with Scripture and disciplined category precision from the assigned chapters.

Evaluation Criteria
- Restoration-process clarity
- Covenantal Reasoning
- Correct use of regeneration language
- Absence of behavioral-only Yada Yahuah
- Readiness for authority and identity studies

Closing Term IV Reflection
"The Third Humanity is not improved humanity—it is transformed humanity."

TERM IV · MONTH 3

THE THREE HUMANITIES™ — IDENTITY, WALK, AUTHORITY, AND FAITHFUL PRESENCE

(Who the Restored Humanity Is and How It Lives)

MODULE OVERVIEW

TERM IV · Month 3 explains how the Third Humanity functions after restoration has occurred.

If Month 1 established why the Third Humanity is required, and Month 2 explained how it is formed, Month 3 reveals how restored humanity lives without reverting to corruption while the world remains divided.

This month corrects confusion between authority and dominance, obedience and legalism, identity and religious affiliation, warfare and coercion, and witness and activism.

Scripture presents the Third Humanity — The Variant $(Y \oplus HW = Y)$ as a restored people living from transformed origin, walking in alignment, operating under delegated authority, and standing as light without adopting the methods of darkness.

By the end of this month, the student will understand that identity precedes behavior, walking reveals origin rather than producing it, authority is delegated rather than seized, obedience is relational rather than institutional, warfare is waged through faithful presence rather than domination, and witness is the natural expression of restored humanity.

This month defines how restored humanity lives before final resurrection.

CHAPTER COVERAGE

The Three Humanities™: — Yahuah's Restoration (Book Five)

- Chapter 3 — The Birth of Yahusha: The Supernatural Invasion of Earth by the Word of Yahuah
- Chapter 4 — The Three Equations of Humanity and the New Seed of Yahuah

in Yahusha

- Chapter 5 — The Ministry of Yahusha: Yahuah in the Flesh Reveals the Eternal Plan of Salvation
- Chapter 6 — The Final Week, the Impalement on the Stake, and the Great Exchange
- Chapter 7 — The Two Priesthoods: Levi vs. Malkiy-Tsedeq — The Eternal Covenant Restored
- Chapter 8 — The Resurrection, the Ascension, and the Birth of the Renewed Covenant People
- Chapter 9 — The Era of the Ruach Qodesh and the Birth of the New Humanity
- Chapter 10 — The Final Truth of the Ruach Qodesh — The Word, the Breath, and the Wisdom of Yahuah in Man

IDENTITY OF THE THIRD HUMANITY
Sons and Daughters by Transformation

PURPOSE OF WEEK 57

Week 57 trains the student to correctly interpret identity within the framework of the Three Humanities. At this stage, identity must no longer be read descriptively or devotionally, but structurally and origin-based. Scripture does not define identity by ethnicity, covenant membership, religious practice, moral status, or social role. Identity is defined exclusively by origin and alignment. The interpretive objective of this week is to transition the student from reading identity as a category one belongs to, toward reading identity as a state of being generated by source. This distinction is critical. Failure at this level results in collapsing the Third Humanity back into Second Humanity logic—where identity is inferred from behavior, affiliation, or law observance.

With the arrival of Yahusha, the plan of salvation decisively shifts. The safeguarding of physical genealogy terminates. In its place, Scripture introduces a spiritual lineage produced through transformation. Week 57 teaches the student how to recognize, trace, and interpret that shift without reverting to flesh-based reasoning.

READ AND INSTRUCTION

- Romans 8:14–17 must be read as an essential statement, not an ethical encouragement. "Sons of Elohiym" is not a title assigned after obedience; it is a declaration of origin verified by Spirit-led existence. The text does not argue for adoption through compliance but identifies sonship as evidence of a new source of life.

- Galatians 3:26–29 must be interpreted as a terminus statement for flesh-based identity. Paul is not dissolving distinctions sociologically; he is declaring that covenant identity is no longer indexed to blood, tribe, or inheritance. The term "seed" must be read post-Messiah as spiritual lineage, not genealogical continuity.

- 1 Peter 2:9–10 must be read diagnostically. The language of "chosen," "called," and "people" functions as identity markers only after transformation has occurred. The passage does not describe how to become the Third Humanity; it describes how the Third Humanity is recognized.

Book Five, Chapters 3 and 4, must be read with strict interpretive discipline. These chapters are not narrative Yada Yahuah; they are origin disclosures. Chapter 3 establishes the moment when Yahuah enters the human equation directly. Chapter 4 provides the governing interpretive apparatus—the Equations—by which all humanity must be classified. Students must resist moral or symbolic readings and maintain structural precision.

Teaching Explanation

Identity in the Three Humanities is never aspirational. It is never achieved, earned, or confirmed by performance. Identity is always received at origin and revealed through alignment. This is the governing interpretive rule of Week 57. The Second Humanity defines identity retrospectively: one acts, therefore one is. The Third Humanity defines identity causally: one is, therefore one acts. The student must learn to recognize this inversion whenever Scripture speaks of sonship, inheritance, obedience, or fruit.

Chapter 4 of Book Five provides the decisive interpretive key. The Three Equations are not metaphors; they are explanatory frameworks for origin. The Third Humanity emerges from Equation 3, carrying both spiritual capacity and fleshly corruption. This explains the instability observed throughout Scripture prior to Messiah. Humanity can respond to Yahuah, yet cannot sustain alignment.

The interpretive rupture occurs with the Variant. When Yahuah enters Equation 3, origin itself is replaced. Identity is no longer anchored in mixed inheritance but in a new Seed whose source is Yahuah Himself. This is why the New Covenant texts consistently define believers as "born of Elohiym," "born from above," or "new creation." These are not ethical descriptions; they are origin statements.

Thus, identity after Yahusha must not be interpreted genealogically—but spiritually. Sonship is not metaphorical adoption into a moral family; it is placement into a new line of being generated by the Ruach. Any interpretation of identity that still relies on ethnicity, institutional authority, Torah observance, or religious status has failed to transition into Third Humanity logic.

KEY TERMS AND DEFINITIONS (WEEK 57)

Third Humanity

Produced by the post-Flood union of Pure Men and Nephilim Women (PM + NW), in which the Pure Man transmits the Ruach and the Nephilim Woman transmits corrupted inheritance, resulting in a partially corrupted, internally divided human condition with the capacity to incline either toward Yahuah or toward evil.

Sonship

Covenantal identity produced by new origin in Yahusha, not conferred through obedience or maintained through performance.

Adoption (Scriptural)

The act of placement into a new spiritual lineage through transformation, not legal reclassification of unchanged nature.

COVENANTAL STUDY TASK

The student must now demonstrate interpretive competence rather than recall.

•The first task is to articulate the identity of the Third Humanity using the Equations framework, without appealing to moral behavior, religious affiliation, or covenant participation as defining markers. Identity must be traced exclusively to origin.

•The second task is to identify where Second Humanity reasoning attempts to reassert itself in discussions of identity—particularly where obedience, law, or tradition are used to validate sonship. These must be flagged as interpretive regressions.

•The final task is to explain how the New Seed in Yahusha (The Variant) terminates flesh-based lineage as a criterion for identity, replacing it with Spirit-generated lineage. The student must demonstrate awareness that this shift is irreversible and governs all New Covenant interpretation.

Scripture and Chapters 3–4 must be cited directly, not paraphrased devotionally.

FINAL THOUGHTS ON WEEK 57

Identity governs alignment. Alignment governs walk. The Third Humanity - The Variant does not behave itself into sonship; it walks because sonship has already been established by origin. Any interpretive system that reverses this order has reverted to Second Humanity logic, regardless of its language.

Week 57 therefore stands as a control point. If identity is misread here, every subsequent reading of obedience, authority, inheritance, and purpose will be distorted.

QUOTE REFLECTION

"You do not walk to become a son.

You walk because origin has already changed."

TERM IV· MONTH 3 — WEEK 58
THE WALK OF ALIGNMENT
Living From a Restored Nature

PURPOSE OF WEEK 58

This week trains the student to correctly interpret "walk" language within the plan of salvation by identifying it as evidentiary, not prescriptive.

Scripture does not use "walk" to command transformation. It uses "walk" to reveal source. At this stage in Yada Yahuah, the student must no longer read walking as spiritual performance, ethical cultivation, or disciplined behavior. Walking functions as diagnostic output — the visible manifestation of restored origin.

Using Book Five, Chapters 5–6, students are trained to interpret the earthly ministry of Yahusha and the Great Exchange as the mechanism that redefines walking itself. Walking is no longer humanity striving toward alignment; it is alignment expressing itself through restored nature.

Week 58 completes the movement from identity (Week 57) to expression, without collapsing expression back into obligation.

READ AND INSTRUCTION

- Micah 6:8
  Walking humbly reflects alignment with Yahuah, not ritual compliance.
- Galatians 5:16–25
  Walking by the Spirit reveals origin through fruit, not effort.
- Ephesians 4:1–6
  The walk reflects calling already received, not identity being pursued.

Student Textbook Reading
The Three Humanities: Yahuah's Restoration — Book Five

- Chapter 5 — The Ministry of Yahusha: Yahuah in the Flesh Reveals the Eternal Plan of Salvation
- Chapter 6 — The Final Week, the Impalement on the Stake, and the Great Exchange

Instructional constraint:

These chapters must be read as origin–expression case studies, not as moral examples or devotional narratives. The student is identifying how walking functions once origin has been replaced.

Teaching Explanation

Walking Is Not a Spiritual Activity — It Is a Revelatory Function

Within Yada Yahuah, "walk" never functions as an instruction to become aligned.

It functions as evidence that alignment has already occurred.

This establishes the governing interpretive rule for the week:

Source determines walk. Walk does not determine source.

Any reading that treats walking as a method of transformation mislocates causality and reintroduces Second Humanity logic. Chapters 5–6 must be interpreted with this causal direction enforced.

Yahusha's Ministry Establishes the Interpretive Baseline for Walking

Chapter 5 must be read as the control specimen for walking language.

Yahusha does not walk rightly because He obeys correctly.

He walks rightly because His origin is uncontaminated.

Where Yahusha walks, alignment appears without effort. Authority flows without enforcement. Obedience exists without instruction. Healing, deliverance, confrontation, and restoration occur as natural outputs of identity, not as disciplines.

The student must learn to interpret Yahusha's ministry as essential inevitability, not exemplary behavior. He does not model how humans should walk; He reveals what walking looks like when origin is restored.

The Failure of Performance-Based Walking Is Exposed, Not Corrected

Throughout Chapter 5, Yahusha repeatedly exposes groups who "walk" meticulously yet remain misaligned:

- Pharisees walk with precision but lack life.

- Sadducees walk with authority but deny the Ruach.
- Temple leadership walks with structure but carries corruption.
- Rome walks with order but produces violence.

The interpretive function here is not critique of morality. It is exposure of false-source walking — movement generated by external systems rather than restored nature.

Students must be trained to recognize that activity is not alignment, and that visible walking may actually conceal deeper misalignment.

The Great Exchange Replaces the Engine of Walking

Chapter 6 must be interpreted as the mechanical replacement of the walk-generator.

At the stake, Yahusha does not merely forgive misalignment; He terminates the old source and installs a new one. This is the decisive interpretive shift.

Before the Great Exchange:

Walking = effort toward obedience under external instruction.

After the Great Exchange:

Walking = manifestation of restored nature under internal alignment.

This distinction is non-negotiable. Any attempt to read post-Messiah walking as improvement, discipline, or gradual conformity collapses the New Covenant back into Second Humanity structures.

Walking by the Spirit Is Evidence, Not Technique

Galatians 5 must be read diagnostically.

Fruit does not appear because effort succeeded.

Fruit appears because root has been healed.

Walking by the Spirit is not a method for producing fruit; it is the observable consequence of Spirit-origin life. The student must be trained to read fruit lists not as goals, but as identity verification markers.

Where fruit is absent, the interpretive question is not discipline failure, but origin confusion.

Alignment Replaces Regulation

Week 58 requires the student to definitively sever walking from enforcement frameworks.

- Empires regulate movement.
- Religions regulate behavior.
- Yahuah restores nature.

Walking in the Third Humanity – The Variant is therefore not obedience under command, but agreement between restored desire and divine instruction. This is why New Covenant texts consistently describe walking as "worthy," "in love," and "by the Spirit" — not because these are aspirational ideals, but because they describe the only possible output of restored origin.

Walk Completes the Identity–Expression Sequence

Week 58 completes the Month 3 interpretive progression without collapsing stages:

Identity (Week 57) establishes who the Third Humanity is.

Walk (Week 58) reveals how that identity expresses itself.

At no point does walking become a means of becoming something else. It is the visible confirmation that transformation has already occurred.

Alignment Focus — Chapters 5 & 6

- Walking language must be read as evidence of source.
- Yahusha's walk reveals uncontaminated origin.
- Performance walking exposes false source.
- The Great Exchange replaces the walk-generator.
- Fruit verifies restoration; it does not cause it.
- Alignment flows from restored desire, not discipline.
- Walk completes identity without reverting to obligation.

KEY TERMS AND DEFINITIONS (WEEK 58)

- Walk
  The visible expression of restored origin, not a method of transformation.
- Alignment

Agreement between renewed desire and divine instruction flowing from new nature.

- Fruit
Observable verification of Spirit-origin life, not evidence of effort.

COVENANTAL STUDY TASK

Pause and complete the following:

•Explain why "walk" language must be read diagnostically rather than prescriptively.

•Demonstrate how Yahusha's ministry establishes walking as essential output.

•Identify how the Great Exchange redefines all post-Messiah walking language.

•Apply the Humanity Equations to preserve causal direction.

Use Scripture and assigned chapters directly.

Avoid performance-based, moral-improvement, or regulation-centered interpretations.

FINAL THOUGHTS ON WEEK 58

Walking does not produce alignment.

Alignment produces walking.

Restored nature expresses itself without coercion.

Humanity Equation Reference:

The Third Humanity — The Variant $(Y \oplus HW = Y)$

QUOTE REFLECTION

"Right walking is not learned — it emerges."

TERM IV· MONTH 3: WEEK 59 — AUTHORITY UNDER HEAVEN
DELEGATED, NOT DOMINATING

PURPOSE OF WEEK 59

This week defines authority as Scripture presents it. Authority is not power over others, but delegated stewardship under heaven.

By examining the shift from Levi to Malkiy-Tsedeq and the resurrection–ascension victory of Yahusha, students see that true authority originates in heaven, operates through covenant order, and is proven by obedience, restraint, and service—not seizure.

READ AND INSTRUCTION

- Luke 10:19–20
  Authority is given for function and victory over spiritual enemies, not pride or self-exaltation.
- Matthew 28:18–20
  All authority belongs to Yahusha by heavenly right; what is delegated flows from His enthroned commission.
- Romans 13:1–4
  Authority operates within divine order; it is not self-created, and it remains accountable to heaven.

The Three Humanities: Yahuah's Restoration — Book Five
- Chapter 7: The Two Priesthoods — Levi vs. Malkiy-Tsedeq
- Chapter 8: The Resurrection, the Ascension, and the Birth of the Renewed Covenant People

Students must read Chapters 7 and 8 in full. These chapters establish that authority is removed from corrupted systems and delegated through the eternal priesthood and kingship of Yahusha.

Teaching Explanation

Scripture reveals two opposing models of authority: seized authority and delegated authority. The Levitical priesthood, though instituted by Yahuah for a fallen nation, was temporary and limited—bound to genealogy, administered by mortal men, and unable to remove sin. It restrained and covered, but could not perfect. It functioned as a shadow until the time of reformation.

Malkiy-Tsedeq reveals the original order: a priesthood older than Levi, higher than Sinai, not based on bloodline, and rooted in eternity. Abraham bows to this order, proving that true authority is recognized, not grabbed. When Yahusha dies, the veil is torn—an act of judicial removal. This signals the termination of the old priestly mediation and the end of the corrupted, usurped priesthood structures. Authority is not reformed; it is replaced.

In Yahusha, authority is enthroned, not campaigned for. He becomes High Priest after the order of Malkiy-Tsedeq—eternal, heavenly, and untransferable. His resurrection proves that death cannot hold the Eternal One. His ascension is the legal proclamation of universal authority: "All authority in heaven and on earth has been given to Me." This is not institutional appointment; it is divine installation.

Therefore the Third Humanity – The Variant does not establish authority structures—it operates within divine order. Authority is exercised under heaven through obedience, restraint, and service. Those who belong to Yahusha function under His commission, never competing for domination. In the renewed covenant people, true authority is measured by submission before action, not power over others.

KEY TERMS AND DEFINITIONS (WEEK 59)

- Authority
  Delegated right to act under divine commission, accountable to heaven.
- Stewardship
  Responsible use of authority for protection, order, and covenant purpose.
- Submission
  Alignment with divine order—not inferiority, but rightful placement under heaven.

COVENANTAL STUDY TASK

Pause your reading and complete the following:

• Explain authority as delegated stewardship under heaven

• Identify abuses that occur when authority is seized or grounded in genealogy, office, or coercion

• Demonstrate how Yahusha's priesthood and ascension define rightful authority

Use Scripture and Chapters 7 and 8 directly.

Avoid models of authority rooted in domination, self-appointment, or institutional supremacy.

FINAL THOUGHTS ON WEEK 59

True authority does not rush to act.

It submits first, then serves.

True authority submits before it acts.

QUOTE REFLECTION

"Authority is proven by restraint."

TERM IV· MONTH 3: WEEK 60 —
WARFARE AND WITNESS IN A DIVIDED WORLD
STANDING WITHOUT BECOMING CORRUPTED

PURPOSE OF WEEK 60

This final week explains how the Third Humanity – The Variant functions in a world that remains divided between light and darkness. Scripture presents warfare and witness without adopting the methods of corruption.

Through the Era of the Ruach Qodesh, students see that victory is achieved not by domination or imitation of darkness, but by standing in restored identity as light-filled witnesses.

READ AND INSTRUCTION

- Ephesians 6:10–18
  Warfare is spiritual, requiring truth, righteousness, faith, and the Word—not fleshly force.
- 2 Corinthians 10:3–5
  The weapons of the Third Humanity – The Variant are divine, dismantling deception without using corrupted methods.
- Matthew 5:14–16
  The restored humanity functions as visible light, bearing witness through transformed life.

The Three Humanities — Book Five

- Chapter 9: The Era of the Ruach Qodesh and the Birth of the New Humanity
- Chapter 10: The Final Truth of the Ruach Qodesh — The Word, the Breath, and the Wisdom of Yahuah in Man

Students must read Chapters 9 and 10 in full. These chapters establish that warfare and witness flow from the indwelling Ruach, reversing Babel and restoring the First Humanity.

Teaching Explanation

After the resurrection and ascension of Yahusha, the conflict does not end—the method changes. The Era of the Ruach Qodesh marks the shift from external confrontation to internal transformation expressed outwardly. The Third Humanity – The Variant does not conquer territory through force; it reclaims people through truth, light, and obedience.

At Pentecost, Babel is reversed. Languages divided by rebellion are unified by the Word. This is spiritual warfare without corruption: truth spoken without coercion, power exercised without domination. The apostles confront principalities, cast out demons, heal the broken, and proclaim Yahusha—not by political takeover or religious control, but by the indwelling Ruach operating through obedient vessels.

Witness is therefore inseparable from warfare. Light exposes darkness simply by remaining light. The Renewed Covenant people do not mimic the tactics of the corrupted seed. They refuse deception, manipulation, violence, and pride. Instead, they stand—clothed in truth, empowered by the Word, guided by wisdom, and restrained by obedience.

Chapter 10 clarifies the foundation of this posture: the Ruach is not a separate entity but the Word, Breath, and Wisdom of Yahuah within man. Warfare is waged through truth spoken, lives aligned, and obedience maintained. The Third Humanity – The Variant overcomes not by becoming darker than the darkness, but by remaining uncontaminated. Standing is victory. Faithfulness is triumph. Witness is warfare.

KEY TERMS AND DEFINITIONS (WEEK 60)

- Spiritual Warfare
  Resistance to deception through truth, obedience, and alignment with the Word.
- Witness
  Visible testimony of restored humanity expressed through light-filled living.

- Restraint
  Refusal to adopt corrupt methods, even when confronting darkness.

COVENANTAL STUDY TASK

Pause your reading and complete the following:

• **Explain spiritual warfare that resists corruption rather than imitating it**

• **Identify how witness functions as a weapon of restoration**

• **Demonstrate how the Ruach enables standing without compromise**

Use Scripture and Chapters 9 and 10 directly.

Avoid models of warfare rooted in coercion, manipulation, or domination.

FINAL THOUGHTS ON WEEK 60

The Third Humanity - The Variant does not win by overpowering the world.

It wins by refusing to become what it confronts.

The Third Humanity - The Variant fights by standing, not conquering.

QUOTE REFLECTION

"Light overcomes darkness by remaining light."

CORE REINFORCEMENT TERM IV· MONTH 3
FROM RESTORED ORIGIN TO FAITHFUL PRESENCE

GOVERNING REALITY OF MONTH 3

Month 3 establishes how the restored humanity functions without reverting to corruption.

The Third Humanity does not:

- strive to become aligned
- build authority structures
- fight darkness with darkness

Instead, it:

- lives from restored origin
- expresses alignment naturally
- functions under delegated authority
- stands as light in a divided world

Month 3 answers one central question:

What does life look like once origin has been restored, identity secured, and authority properly delegated—while the world remains broken?

The Fixed Causal Chain (Non-Negotiable)
Month 3 locks in the irreversible order of causality:

- Identity is established by origin (Week 57)
- Walk emerges as evidence of that origin (Week 58)
- Authority is delegated under heaven, not seized (Week 59)
- Warfare & Witness occur through faithful presence, not corruption (Week 60)

Any interpretation that reverses this order has collapsed back into Second Humanity logic.

Identity Is Not Achieved — It Is Received

Week 57 established the foundation:

- Identity is genealogical (spiritually), not behavioral
- Sonship is not validated by obedience
- Alignment flows from origin, not aspiration

Core Reinforcement:

You do not act to become.

You act because you already are.

Walking Is Diagnostic, Not Prescriptive

Week 58 corrected all "walk" language:

- Walking does not produce alignment
- Walking reveals alignment
- Fruit verifies source; it does not cause it

Core Reinforcement:

Right walking is not learned.

It emerges when origin is healed.

Authority Is Delegated, Not Generated

Week 59 permanently redefined authority:

- Authority originates in heaven
- Authority is installed, not campaigned for
- Authority is proven by restraint, obedience, and service

Levi represents temporary restraint.

Malkiy-Tsedeq represents eternal installation.

Core Reinforcement:

True authority submits before it acts.

Anything seized is already corrupted.

Warfare Is Standing, Not Domination

Week 60 completed the sequence:

- Warfare does not end after resurrection — its method changes
- The Third Humanity – The Variant does not conquer systems
- It reclaims people through truth, light, and witness

Pentecost reverses Babel without force.

Light exposes darkness without imitation.

Core Reinforcement:

The Third Humanity – The Variant does not win by overpowering the world.

It wins by refusing to become what it confronts.

The Unifying Principle of Month 3

Across all four weeks, one rule governs everything:

Restored origin produces aligned presence — not managed performance.

- Identity governs walk
- Walk governs function
- Function operates under heaven
- Warfare is won by remaining uncontaminated

Standing is not passivity.

Standing is fidelity.

Final Anchor Statement (Month 3)

Month 3 permanently trains the student to recognize this truth:

The Third Humanity – The Variant does not fix the world by force.

It reveals the Kingdom by remaining aligned.

Faithfulness is victory.

Presence is warfare.

Light wins by being light.

TERM IV · MONTH 4
THE THREE HUMANITIES™ — CONSUMMATION, SEPARATION, AND ETERNAL ALIGNMENT
(How Restoration Is Completed and Secured Forever)

MODULE OVERVIEW

TERM IV · Month 4 brings The Three Humanities™ to its final instructional completion.

If Month 1 established the necessity of restoration,

Month 2 revealed the mechanics of redemption,

and Month 3 defined the identity, walk, authority, and witness of the Variant,

then Month 4 explains how restoration is finished, protected, and made irreversible.

This month resolves every remaining open question within the Restoration framework.

Students are no longer asked:

- Can restoration succeed?
- Will corruption return?
- Is judgment compatible with mercy?

Month 4 establishes that restoration cannot remain incomplete, cannot coexist with corruption, and cannot remain unsecured.

GOVERNING FOCUS OF MONTH 4

This month trains the student to understand that:

- Restoration requires separation
- Separation requires judgment
- Judgment enables resurrection
- Resurrection enables inheritance
- Inheritance stabilizes eternity

Nothing in creation reaches permanence without boundary enforcement.

CORE DISTINCTIONS CLARIFIED IN MONTH 4

Month 4 resolves widespread misunderstandings by establishing that:

- Mercy restores individuals; judgment restores order
- Coexistence is temporary; separation is permanent
- The Variant is real restoration, but not final completion
- Resurrection is not optional; it is required
- Inheritance is not reward-based; it is nature-based
- Eternity cannot contain mixture, corruption, or probation

CHAPTER COVERAGE — MONTH 4

The Three Humanities™ — Yahuah's Restoration (Book Five)

- Chapter 11 — The Growth of the Renewed Covenant People and the War Against Darkness
- Chapter 12 — The Final Condition of Humanity Before the Second Coming of the Mashiyach
- Chapter 13 — The Generation That Broke the Four Pillars
- Chapter 14 — The Redemption of Creation
- Chapter 15 — The Final Judgment and the End of the Seed War
- Chapter 16 — The New Heaven and the New Earth — Yahuah Dwells With Humanity Again

These chapters are not read devotionally or independently.

They function as a single restoration sequence, moving from escalation → separation → judgment → resurrection → renewal → eternal stability.

WHAT MONTH 4 COMPLETES

By the end of this month, the student will understand:

- Why the Flood ended the Second Humanity, but not its spiritual legacy
- Why the Third Humanity (Mixed Humanity) continues until final cleansing
- Why the Variant exists within the Third Humanity, not outside it
- Why final judgment removes all remaining corruption
- Why resurrection restores humanity to the First Humanity

- Why creation itself must be released, not merely repaired
- Why eternity cannot collapse back into rebellion

POSITION OF MONTH 4 IN THE PROGRAM

Month 4 is the last instructional month of The Three Humanities™.

After this point:

- No new framework is introduced
- No new equations are added
- No unresolved categories remain

What follows in TERM V is not instruction — it is demonstration, deduction, and defense.

MONTH 4 DECLARATION

Restoration does not end when sin is forgiven.

It ends when corruption is removed.

Restoration does not succeed when mercy is offered.

It succeeds when order is secured.

Restoration is not complete until humanity, creation, and authority

are aligned permanently under Yahuah.

This month explains how that completion occurs.

TERM IV· MONTH 4 — WEEK 61
FINAL SEPARATION
Why Restoration Cannot Remain Open-Ended

PURPOSE OF WEEK 61

Week 61 trains the student to correctly interpret separation language in Scripture within the completed arc of the Three Humanities.

At this stage in Yada Yahuah, separation must no longer be read as:

- punitive retaliation
- emotional wrath
- divine impatience
- failure of mercy

Instead, separation must be interpreted structurally, as the final protective action required once restoration has reached its limit.

Week 61 does not introduce a new doctrine.

It completes a trajectory already established:

- Identity restored (Weeks 57–58)
- Authority delegated (Week 59)
- Warfare restrained (Week 60)

Now the student must understand why coexistence between restoration and corruption cannot continue indefinitely without collapse.

This week teaches why separation becomes necessary — not as threat, but as outcome.

READ AND INSTRUCTION

Matthew 13:36–43

Messiah explains the Wheat and the Tares not as moral contrast, but as a timed structural process. Growth permits coexistence; completion forbids it.

Malachi 4

The prophetic close of the former age establishes irreversible distinction as the final condition of restoration.

Revelation 20

Final judgment is revealed not as rage, but as containment — securing renewed creation from return of corruption.

Student Textbook Reading

The Three Humanities — Book Five

- Chapter 11 — The Growth of the Renewed Covenant People and the War Against Darkness
- Chapter 12 — The Final Condition of Humanity Before the Second Coming of the Mashiyach

Instructional Constraint

These texts must be read as restoration-limit disclosures, not as apocalyptic fear material or symbolic abstractions. The student is identifying why continued coexistence eventually undermines restoration itself.

Teaching Explanation

Separation Is Not Introduced — It Emerges

Separation does not appear suddenly at the end of Scripture. It emerges gradually as restoration advances.

In early stages, mercy gathers.

In middle stages, truth clarifies.

In final stages, separation protects.

Week 61 establishes the governing interpretive rule:

What mercy gathers, separation must eventually secure.

Any reading that treats separation as optional misunderstands restoration as infinite tolerance rather than structural healing.

Matthew 13 Defines the Limit of Coexistence

Messiah's explanation of the Wheat and the Tares is not moral instruction; it is process disclosure.

He explicitly rejects every alternative outcome:

- tares are not corrected
- tares are not merged
- tares are not slowly absorbed

The decisive phrase is "at the harvest."

Growth requires shared space.

Harvest requires distinction.

If coexistence continued past harvest:

- wheat would be compromised
- roots would be entangled
- restoration would regress

Thus, separation is not hostility toward tares; it is preservation of wheat.

Parallel Growth Clarifies, Not Confuses (Book Five, Chapter 11)

Chapter 11 reveals that restoration and corruption grow simultaneously.

This is not failure of the Renewed Covenant people.

It is exposure of final alignment.

As truth spreads:

- deception intensifies
- false teachers multiply
- apostasy clarifies itself

Week 61 teaches the student that clarity precedes separation.

Without clarity, separation would be unjust.

With clarity complete, separation becomes necessary.

Malachi 4 Ends Process Language

Malachi 4 does not speak in developmental terms.

It speaks in outcome language.

The righteous are healed and preserved.

The wicked are removed entirely.

This is not gradual correction.

It is final distinction.

The interpretive principle is decisive:

Restoration culminates in polarity, not dialogue.

Any Yada Yahuah that insists on eternal process denies the prophetic closure Yahuah Himself announces.

Revelation 20 Secures Restoration Against Return

Revelation 20 must be read structurally, not emotionally.

The final judgment accomplishes three functions:

- corrupt authority is terminated
- irreparable seed is removed
- renewed creation is secured

The lake of fire functions as containment, not vengeance.

Without this containment:

- deception could re-enter
- rebellion could resurface
- restoration would remain provisional

Week 61 establishes that security is an act of mercy toward the restored.

Chapter 12 Explains Why Delay Can No Longer Continue

Chapter 12 describes a world that has:

- lost the Name
- confused identity
- normalized corruption
- returned to Noach-pattern conditions

At this point, continued coexistence no longer protects growth — it threatens survival.

Separation becomes necessary not because mercy failed, but because mercy has finished its gathering work.

Separation Completes the Restoration Arc

Week 61 completes the causal sequence without contradiction:

- Mercy gathers
- Truth clarifies
- Alignment forms
- Corruption is exposed
- Separation secures

Restoration is not complete when rebellion is restrained.

It is complete when rebellion is removed from access.

Alignment Focus — Chapters 11 & 12

- Parallel growth clarifies final alignment.
- Harvest marks the end of coexistence.
- Prophetic closure replaces process language.
- Final judgment secures restored creation.
- Separation protects what mercy healed.

KEY TERMS AND DEFINITIONS (WEEK 61)

- Separation
  The final protective act that secures restored creation once alignment is complete.
- Harvest
  The structural moment when coexistence ends and distinction becomes necessary.
- Containment
  Removal of irreparable corruption to prevent return and preserve restoration.

COVENANTAL STUDY TASK

Pause and complete the following:

•Explain why restoration cannot remain indefinitely open-ended
•Demonstrate how Matthew 13 defines separation as preservation
•Identify how Chapter 11 reveals clarity before separation
•Explain why Chapter 12 marks the limit of mercy's delay
•Defend Revelation 20 as containment, not retaliation

Use Scripture and Book Five Chapters 11–12 directly.
Avoid emotional framing, universalist assumptions, or coexistence Yada Yahuah.

FINAL THOUGHTS ON WEEK 61

Mercy begins restoration.

Truth completes alignment.

Separation secures the healed creation forever.

Restoration is not threatened by separation.

It collapses without it.

Humanity Equation Reference:

The Third Humanity – The Variant $(Y \oplus HW = Y)$

QUOTE REFLECTION

"Mercy gathers the restored.

Separation keeps them restored."

TERM IV· MONTH 4 — WEEK 62
JUDGMENT AS RESTORATION'S BOUNDARY
Justice That Secures Renewal

PURPOSE OF WEEK 62

Week 62 trains the student to correctly interpret judgment language within the plan of salvation by identifying judgment as restoration's boundary, not restoration's contradiction.

Scripture does not present judgment as emotional rage or divine instability. Judgment functions as the moment when mercy is no longer negotiating with corruption and restoration moves from invitation to enforcement. Mercy restores persons. Judgment restores order. Without judgment, restoration remains reversible because corruption retains return access.

Using Book Five, Chapters 13–14, students are trained to read the final generation not as a merely "sinful world," but as a world that dismantles the very pillars that make repentance intelligible. At that stage, judgment is not optional—it becomes the only remaining mechanism by which renewal is protected.

Week 62 follows Week 61 without collapsing into fear or punishment framing. Separation was established as necessary. Week 62 explains how separation is enforced so restoration becomes irreversible.

READ AND INSTRUCTION

- Yashayahu (Isaiah) 26
  Judgment is shown as instruction through reality: when truth is rejected long enough, consequences become the teacher.
- Rómĕos (Romans) 2
  Judgment is shown as impartial assessment: identity, lineage, and reputation do not exempt anyone; response to truth is the measure.
- Apokálypsis (Revelation) 19
  Judgment is shown as creation being reclaimed: heaven rejoices because deception ends and order is restored.

Student Textbook Reading

The Three Humanities: Yahuah's Restoration — Book Five

- Chapter 13 — The Generation That Broke the Four Pillars
- Chapter 14 — The Redemption of Creation

Instructional constraint:

These chapters must be read as boundary–renewal disclosures, not end-time sensation or emotional punishment material. The student is identifying why judgment becomes required once covenant reference points have been dismantled.

Teaching Explanation

Judgment Is Not the Opposite of Mercy — It Is Mercy Securing the Future

Within Yada Yahuah, mercy is not permission for corruption to remain active forever. Mercy gathers what can be healed. Judgment prevents what cannot be healed from re-infecting what has been restored.

This establishes the governing interpretive rule for the week:

Mercy restores people. Judgment secures the restored world.

Any reading that treats judgment as "against restoration" mislocates judgment's function and turns restoration into endless probation.

Isaiah 26 Defines Judgment as Instruction by Reality, Not Emotional Retaliation

Isaiah does not present judgment as uncontrolled anger. Isaiah presents judgment as the remaining teacher once instruction has been rejected.

The passage teaches that when judgments are active in the earth, the world learns righteousness—not because hearts suddenly become pure, but because reality becomes unavoidable. Mercy invites alignment. Judgment enforces alignment. Instruction shifts from invitation to consequence.

The student must learn to read judgment as structural correction: not persuasion by words, but instruction by outcomes once words are despised.

Romans 2 Establishes Judgment as Impartial Alignment Assessment

Romans 2 removes three false shelters that humans commonly trust:

- identity-based immunity
- institutional protection
- reputation-based exemption

The text defines judgment as universal accountability measured by response to truth. The student must recognize that this is essential to restoration logic: if judgment were biased, the restored order would be unstable and unjust.

Romans 2 is therefore not an argument about who is "better." It is an announcement that no created category can override accountability to Yahuah. Judgment is structural and universal because restoration is structural and universal.

Revelation 19 Shows Judgment as Praise-Worthy Because It Ends What Mercy Could Not Heal

Revelation 19 presents a result that modern thinking often cannot tolerate: heaven rejoices at judgment.

Why does heaven rejoice? Because judgment ends deception, breaks corrupt systems, and restores moral order to creation. The rejoicing is not delight in pain; it is relief that corruption no longer has authority to damage, seduce, and destroy.

The interpretive function is decisive: Revelation 19 frames judgment as the termination of chaos. Judgment is not disorder; it is the end of disorder.

Chapter 13 Explains Why Judgment Becomes Inevitable: The Four Pillars Are Broken

Chapter 13 identifies the final generation not as people who merely sin, but as a civilization that breaks the framework that makes repentance possible.

The Four Pillars named in the chapter are presented as covenant reference points:

1.   Torah rejected — lawlessness normalized, truth loses definition
2.   Shabbath erased — covenant sign removed, identity unmarked

3.   Feasts replaced — prophetic calendar lost, redemption seasons unread

4.   Name corrupted — authority and identity severed at the root

This is not ignorance. It is structural rejection of alignment itself. The student must interpret this as the moment when mercy's invitation has no shared language left. When reference points are dismantled, restoration cannot be negotiated because the very terms of return have been erased.

This is why judgment becomes unavoidable: not because Yahuah runs out of patience, but because the world removes the last anchors that allow repentance to be understood.

Chapter 14 Defines Judgment as Redemption Applied to Creation

Chapter 14 corrects the final misunderstanding: judgment is not the end of redemption; it is redemption enforced upon the created order.

This chapter presents judgment as the mechanism by which creation is reclaimed from corruption. The removal of the beast system, false authority, and deceiving power is not a side issue—it is how creation becomes safe for restored life.

The student must learn to read judgment as restoration's surgical act toward creation: what cannot be healed is terminated so what can be healed can remain healed.

Judgment Enforces the Boundary Established by Separation

Week 61 established that coexistence cannot continue into completion. Week 62 establishes that the boundary must be enforced or it will be violated.

If judgment does not occur:

- mercy is exploited
- restoration stays reversible
- corruption keeps return access

Therefore, judgment is not an optional doctrine added to restoration. Judgment is the enforcement mechanism that makes restoration permanent.

Alignment Focus — Chapters 13 & 14

- Judgment is structural, not emotional.
- Isaiah shows judgment as instruction through reality.
- Romans establishes universal accountability without exemption.
- Revelation shows judgment reclaiming order and ending deception.
- Chapter 13 shows why mercy loses shared reference points.
- Chapter 14 shows judgment as redemption applied to creation.
- Boundary enforcement secures irreversible renewal.

Key Terms and Definitions (Week 62)

- Judgment
  Boundary enforcement that ends corruption's access and secures restored order.
- Justice
  Rightful alignment assessment applied universally, without exemption or bias.
- Boundary
  The point where mercy's invitation ends and restoration is protected through enforcement.

COVENANTAL STUDY TASK

Pause and complete the following:

•Explain why judgment is restoration's boundary rather than restoration's contradiction

•Demonstrate how Isaiah 26 frames judgment as instruction through reality

•Demonstrate how Romans 2 destroys identity-based exemption models

•Explain why Revelation 19 treats judgment as order restored

•Use Chapters 13–14 to show why judgment becomes unavoidable in the final generation

•Present how judgment restores creation by enforcing cleansing and protection

Use Scripture and assigned chapters directly.

Avoid emotional framing, punishment-centered models, individual-only morality, or coexistence assumptions.

FINAL THOUGHTS ON WEEK 62

Mercy gathers what can be healed.

Judgment protects what has been healed.

Without judgment, restoration remains temporary.

With judgment, restoration becomes irreversible.

Humanity Equation Reference:

The Third Humanity — The Variant $(Y \oplus HW = Y)$

QUOTE REFLECTION

"Judgment is mercy protecting tomorrow."

TERM IV· MONTH 4 — WEEK 63
RENEWAL AND CONSUMMATION OF RESTORATION
Redemption of Creation — The End of the Seed War

PURPOSE OF WEEK 63

Week 63 trains the student to correctly interpret restoration language at its completed stage by identifying restoration not as repair, restraint, or improvement, but as creational release.

Up to this point in Term IV:

- Week 61 established why separation is necessary
- Week 62 established how judgment enforces that separation
- Week 63 now establishes what reality becomes once separation and judgment have fully accomplished their work.

Scripture does not present restoration as a repaired version of a broken world. It presents restoration as the termination of corruption's authority, the end of the Seed War, and the release of creation into its original design.

Using Book Five, Chapters 15–16, students are trained to read the end of history not as escalation, but as resolution. This week answers the final interpretive question of the Three Humanities framework:

What does creation look like when corruption is no longer possible?

READ AND INSTRUCTION

- Rómĕos (Romans) 8:18–23
  Creation is revealed as a participant in redemption, awaiting release from imposed corruption, not moral improvement.
- Yashayahu (Isaiah) 11
  Harmony in creation is revealed as structural realignment after corrupt authority is removed, not symbolic poetry.
- 1 Korínthios (1 Corinthians) 15
  The final transfer of authority is revealed, culminating in the abolition of death itself.

- Apokálypsis (Revelation) 21–22
  The final state of restored creation is revealed: New Heaven, New Earth, New Yarushalayim, and Yahuah dwelling with humanity.

Student Textbook Reading
The Three Humanities — Book Five
- Chapter 15 — The Final Judgment & the End of the Seed War
- Chapter 16 — The New Heaven and the New Earth — Yahuah Dwells With Humanity Again

Instructional constraint:
These chapters must be read as resolution disclosures, not future speculation or symbolic imagery. The student is identifying how restoration functions once corruption, rebellion, and hybrid contamination are fully removed.

Teaching Explanation
The Seed War Explains Why History Could Not End Earlier
Chapter 15 establishes the governing reality behind all biblical history:
Two seeds cannot coexist forever.

From Bereshith onward, humanity exists under unresolved conflict between:
- the Seed aligned with Yahuah
- the seed of rebellion introduced through corruption

This conflict was not merely moral or ideological. It was creational, genetic, spiritual, and systemic. Covenants managed it. Mercy delayed it. Judgment restrained it. But management is not resolution.

As long as corrupted seed, hybrid influence, and rebellious authority retained existence, creation could not stabilize. History therefore could not conclude earlier—not because Yahuah delayed victory, but because the conflict itself had not yet been terminated at the source.

Week 63 assumes that termination has now occurred.

Chapter 15 — Judgment Ends the Seed War, Not Merely Its Symptoms
Chapter 15 clarifies a critical finality: human history ends at the return of Yahusha.

At His appearing:
- The Variant (the restored portion of the Third Humanity) is transformed into the perfected First Humanity
- the corrupted seed is destroyed in the second death
- no mixed humanity remains
- no corrupted lineage survives
- no human rebellion continues

This is not postponement. This is termination.

The Seed War among humanity ends permanently because the reproductive capacity of rebellion is removed. Judgment does not merely defeat opposition; it eliminates its ability to exist again.

Romans 8 — Creation Is Released, Not Repaired

Romans 8 reframes restoration at a world level. Creation is not scenery. Creation is enslaved.

Decay, entropy, and death are not neutral conditions; they are imposed consequences of corrupted authority. Creation "groans" not because it is broken beyond design, but because it is restrained from operating according to its original order.

Once judgment removes corruption:
- decay loses jurisdiction
- entropy is no longer enforced
- death is no longer inevitable

Restoration therefore moves beyond humanity into the restoration of created order under Yahuah. Creation does not improve morally. It is freed structurally.

Isaiah 11 — Harmony Is the Result of Authority Shift

Isaiah 11 must be read as post-conflict reality, not poetic symbolism. Predation ends. Violence ceases. Fear dissolves. These changes do not occur because creatures are trained differently, but because the law of corruption that governed behavior is no longer active.

This is not reform. It is creational realignment.

When corrupt authority is removed:
- altered natures stabilize
- aggression loses its driver
- death-instinct disappears

Creation behaves differently because creation is governed differently.

Chapter 16 — Restoration Is Release Into Original Design

Chapter 16 marks the turning point of the entire Institute.

Restoration here is not:
- repair of damage
- restraint of evil
- moral improvement

Restoration is release.

Release means:
- authority chains are removed
- foreign law is annulled
- original design resumes

This is why:
- New Heaven and New Earth appear
- New Yarushalayim descends
- no temple is required
- no sun or moon is needed
- no death, pain, or curse remains

Creation does not strive. Creation is freed.

1 Corinthians 15 — Death Must Be Removed for Restoration to Stabilize
The final enemy is not sin.

The final enemy is death.

Death is corruption's enforcement mechanism. As long as death exists:

- fear persists
- decay continues
- instability remains possible

When death is abolished:

- corruption has no leverage
- rebellion has no consequence system
- restoration becomes irreversible

This is the final transfer of authority. Messiah reigns until all enemies—including death—are removed, then authority returns fully to the Father. This is not loss of power; it is completion of purpose.

Restoration Is Creational Completion, Not Moral Success

Week 63 requires the student to abandon all partial frameworks.

Restoration is not:

- humanity behaving better
- sin being managed
- evil being restrained

Restoration is:

- corruption made impossible
- rebellion unable to exist
- creation released into original order

The Seed War does not pause.

It ends.

Alignment Focus — Chapters 15 & 16

- The Seed War required final termination.
- Judgment ends reproductive rebellion.
- Human history concludes at Yahusha's return.
- Creation is enslaved under corruption.
- Release follows authority removal.

- Harmony results from restored order.
- Death's abolition secures permanence.
- Restoration becomes irreversible completion.

Key Terms and Definitions (Week 63)

- Restoration

  The irreversible release of creation into its original design once corruption is removed.

- Seed War

  The creational conflict between aligned seed and corrupted seed that ends with final judgment.

- Release

  The removal of imposed corruption allowing creation to function as designed.

COVENANTAL STUDY TASK

Pause and complete the following:

- ***Explain the Seed War and why it must end, not be managed***
- ***Demonstrate how judgment resolves corruption rather than restraining it***
- ***Show how creation itself is redeemed using Romans 8 and Chapter 16***
- ***Explain why death must be removed for eternal stability***
- ***Articulate restoration as creational completion, not moral achievement***

Use Scripture and assigned chapters directly.

Avoid speculation, symbolism-only readings, cyclical struggle models, or regression to earlier-stage frameworks.

FINAL THOUGHTS ON WEEK 63

Restoration is not complete when enemies are defeated.

It is complete when their ability to exist is removed.

The Seed War does not pause.

It ends.

Creation does not survive restoration.

It is reborn.

Humanity Equation Reference:

The Third Humanity — The Variant ($Y \oplus HW = Y$)

QUOTE REFLECTION

"Restoration is not repair.

It is release."

TERM IV· MONTH 4 — WEEK 64
THE COMPLETE HUMANITY MAP
Creation → Corruption → Restoration → Eternal First Humanity
Equations, History, and the Fulfillment of Yahuah's Purpose

PURPOSE OF WEEK 64

Week 64 completes the teaching of The Three Humanities™ by presenting the entire restoration framework as one continuous, unified map.

This week does not introduce new doctrine.

It integrates everything already taught from Term I through Term IV into a single interpretive structure that the student can now hold, trace, and defend.

The student is no longer learning isolated stages.

The student is learning to see the whole.

Week 64 trains the student to:

- Trace humanity from creation to eternity without contradiction
- Maintain correct causal direction across all phases
- Preserve the meaning of every Humanity Equation
- Distinguish clearly between:
    - corruption
    - mixture
    - restoration
    - transformation
- Understand why judgment, separation, and resurrection are required — not optional

This is the final instructional week of The Three Humanities.

Nothing follows except fulfillment and thesis work.

READ AND INSTRUCTION

- Genesis 1–6
  Creation, fall, corruption, and the beginning of the Seed War
- Matthew 24:37–39

The days of Noach as the pattern for the end
- John 20:22
  The breath of restoration — the Variant begins
- 1 Corinthians 15:50–57
  Transformation from corruptible to incorruptible
- Revelation 21–22
  Restored creation and eternal dwelling with Yahuah

STUDENT TEXTBOOK READING

The Three Humanities™: Yahuah's Restoration — Book Five

- Chapters 1–16 (Integrated Review)
- No single chapter governs this week
- The entire book functions as one completed system

Instructional Constraint:

All texts must be read structurally, not devotionally.

The student is tracing causal continuity, not extracting inspiration.

Teaching Explanation

1. The First Humanity — Origin Without Corruption

Humanity Equation

$Y + A = FH$

Meaning (Fixed):

Yahuah $\rightarrow$ Adam = First Humanity

Spirit-first, pure, incorruptible origin

The First Humanity is created directly by the Ruach of Yahuah.

Spirit precedes flesh.

Humanity is aligned, unified, and uncontaminated.

Key Characteristics

- Pure spiritual origin
- No demonic influence
- No genetic corruption

- Direct fellowship with Yahuah
- Created for eternal communion

The fall introduces mortality and separation — not hybridization.

Corruption does not fully manifest until external interference occurs.

Closure of the First Humanity

The descent of the Watchers marks the end of this phase.

From this point forward, humanity is no longer isolated from celestial rebellion.

2. The Second Humanity — Hybrid Corruption Introduced

Humanity Equations

    1. $AW + HW = N$

    Angel Watchers + Human Women = Nephilim

    2. $NM + PW = N$

Nephilim Men + Pure Women = Continued Hybridization

The Second Humanity is not fallen humanity — it is altered humanity.

Key Characteristics

- Genetic corruption
- Hybrid bodies
- Forbidden knowledge
- Violence and domination
- Active destruction of the pure seed

This humanity threatens the extinction of Yahuah's creation plan.

The Flood — Corrected Understanding

The Flood:

- Terminates the dominance of the Second Humanity
- Destroys hybrid bodies
- Preserves the creation through Noach
- Does not eliminate all Nephilim genetic continuity

At least one Nephilim bloodline survives, allowing corruption to continue post-Flood.

Nephilim spirits remain confined and later operate as unclean spirits.

This is non-negotiable, as it explains:

- Post-Flood giants
- Canaanite hybrid nations
- Ongoing Seed War conditions

3. The Third Humanity — Mixed Humanity

Humanity Equation

PM + NW = MH

Meaning:

Pure Men + Nephilim Women = Mixed Humanity

This is not restoration.

This is biological humanity restored, but spiritually damaged.

Key Characteristics:

- Flesh-first nature
- Spiritually dead condition
- Internal conflict
- Vulnerable to demonic influence
- Incapable of approaching Yahuah independently

This humanity:

- Populates the post-Flood world
- Builds Babel (Nephilim bloodline)
- Forms empires
- Receives Torah
- Produces prophets
- Remains unable to restore itself

Historical Span

Post-Flood → End of the Age

The Third Humanity continues until final cleansing.

It does not end with Yahusha.

This is the humanity that:

- Yahusha enters
- the Variant emerges from
- will ultimately be separated and judged

4. The Third Humanity — The Variant (Transformation Begins)

Humanity Restoration Equation

$$Y \oplus HW = Y$$

Meaning:

Yahuah (Ruach) + Human Woman (Miryam) = Yahusha

The New Spiritual Humanity is born

This is the turning point of all history.

Through Yahusha:

- Ruach is restored
- understanding is opened
- rebirth becomes possible

Defining Moment:

"He breathed on them and said, 'Receive rûach Qôdesh.'" — *John 20:22*

The Variant is:

- still living within corruptible flesh
- internally conflicted
- spiritually alive
- awaiting transformation

The Variant exists within the Third Humanity, not apart from it.

5. The Return to the First Humanity — Restoration Completed

Final Humanity Equation

$$Y + RT = FH$$

Meaning:

Yahusha (the perfected Variant) + Resurrection Transformation

= First Humanity Restored

This is not regression.

This is completion.

Key Characteristics:

- Incorruptible bodies
- No death
- No mixture
- No internal conflict
- Eternal communion with Yahuah

What Adam lost is restored — and surpassed — through Yahusha.

The Variant becomes the First Humanity in fullness.

System Integration

- The Flood restrains corruption, it does not resolve it
- Torah reveals alignment, it does not restore nature
- Yahusha restores the Ruach, but transformation awaits resurrection
- Judgment removes what cannot be healed
- Resurrection completes what restoration began

Every stage is necessary.

Nothing is redundant.

Nothing is skipped.

Key Terms Week 64

- The First Humanity (Y + A = FH): Yahuah → Adam = First Humanity
- Spirit-first, pure, incorruptible origin. The First Humanity is created directly by the Ruach of Yahuah.
- The Second Humanity (AW + HW = N) & NM + PW = N: Angel Watchers + Human Women = Nephilim and Nephilim Men + Pure Women = Continued Hybridization. The Second Humanity is not fallen humanity — it is altered humanity.
- The Third Humanity (PM + NW = MH): Pure Men + Nephilim Women = Mixed Humanity. This is not restoration. This is biological humanity restored, but

spiritually damaged.

- The Third Humanity — The Variant (Y $\oplus$ HW = Y): Yahuah (Ruach) + Human Woman (Miryam) = Yahusha. The New Spiritual Humanity is born
- The Return to the First Humanity (Y + RT = FH): Yahusha (the perfected Variant) + Resurrection Transformation = First Humanity Restored

COVENANTAL STUDY TASK

The student must now demonstrate system-level mastery.

Required Demonstration

- *Trace all five humanities in correct order*
- *Preserve the meaning of each equation*
- *Explain why the Third Humanity persists until the end*
- *Distinguish clearly between Mixed Humanity and the Variant*
- *Defend resurrection as necessary for final restoration*

Guardrails: No emotional framing, No speculative chronology, No collapsing stages, No metaphor substitution

FINAL THOUGHTS — WEEK 64

The story of humanity is not random.

It is structured.

Creation was not abandoned.

It was guided.

Corruption did not win.

It was contained.

Restoration did not rush.

It unfolded.

The First Humanity was not lost forever.

It was delayed — until Yahusha.

Humanity does not end in mixture.

It ends in restoration.

RESTORATION COMPLETED THROUGH SEPARATION, JUDGMENT, TRANS-FORMATION, AND INHERITANCE

TERM IV · Month 4 completes the teaching of The Three Humanities™ by bringing the entire Plan of Restoration to its necessary conclusion. This month does not expand the framework—it finishes it.

Up to this point, the student has learned:

- why humanity required restoration
- how corruption entered and persisted
- what Yahusha restored through the Ruach
- where the Variant exists within mixed humanity

Month 4 now establishes the final truth:

Restoration is not complete until corruption is permanently removed, transformation is finished, and alignment becomes irreversible.

This month trains the student to understand that restoration is not sentimental, gradual, or endless. It is directional, decisive, and terminal.

WHAT MONTH 4 RESOLVES

Month 4 resolves four critical questions that cannot remain open if restoration is to stand:

1.Why coexistence between alignment and corruption cannot continue

2.Why judgment is required to secure restoration

3.Why resurrection is necessary to complete transformation

4.Why inheritance is based on restored nature, not moral effort

These are not philosophical questions.

They are structural necessities within the Plan of Yahuah.

Restoration Requires Separation

Month 4 establishes that coexistence between restoration and corruption is a temporary allowance, not an eternal design.

Mercy gathers.

But mercy alone cannot protect what has been restored.

As long as corruption remains present, restoration remains vulnerable.

Therefore, separation is not an act of rejection—it is an act of preservation.

Separation is the moment when restoration moves from possibility to security.

Judgment Is the Enforcement of Restoration

Judgment is not introduced as retaliation, anger, or punishment.

It is revealed as boundary enforcement.

Where mercy invites alignment, judgment enforces it.

Where mercy restores individuals, judgment restores order.

Without judgment:
- corruption retains return rights
- deception remains possible
- restoration becomes reversible

Month 4 clarifies that judgment is not the opposite of mercy—it is mercy's final protective form.

Transformation Is Not Finished Until Resurrection

The Variant represents real restoration, but not final completion.

As long as humanity remains in corruptible flesh:
- death retains authority
- internal conflict persists
- corruption remains externally present

Month 4 confirms that resurrection is not an upgrade—it is a necessity.

Only resurrection removes corruption at the structural level.

Transformation that does not culminate in resurrection is incomplete by definition.

Inheritance Is Revealed, Not Awarded

Inheritance is not given as a reward for effort.

It is disclosed as confirmation of nature.

Those who inherit restored creation do so because they belong to it.

They are aligned, restored, transformed, and incorruptible.

There is no future test.

There is no further probation.

There is no second fall.

Month 4 closes the idea that eternity contains risk, instability, or renewed rebellion.

What Month 4 Permanently Establishes

By the end of Month 4, the following truths are fixed and non-negotiable within **Restoration Yada Yahuah:**

- Corruption does not evolve into alignment
- Mixture cannot inherit eternity
- Restoration requires removal of what cannot be healed
- Judgment secures what mercy restores
- Resurrection completes what the Ruach begins
- The Variant becomes the First Humanity in fullness
- Creation itself is released once corruption ends

Nothing further is required doctrinally.

Why Month 4 Is the Necessary End of Instruction

The Three Humanities™ framework is now complete.

The student has been given:

- the equations
- the history
- the causal logic
- the restoration arc

From this point forward, the task is no longer learning new structure, but demonstrating mastery of the whole.

This is why TERM V does not introduce doctrine.

It requires deduction, defense, and articulation.

Final Reinforcement Statement

Yahuah did not lose His creation to corruption.

He guided it through corruption toward completion.

Restoration does not end with forgiveness.

It ends with transformation.

The Plan of Yahuah does not pause in mixture.

It resolves in alignment.

The Three Humanities do not conclude in struggle.

They conclude in the restored First Humanity — eternal, incorruptible, and complete.

From Instruction to Demonstration

TERM IV concludes the instructional phase of The Three Humanities™.

Across its progression, the student has been given:

- the complete Restoration framework
- the full Humanity Equations
- the historical arc from Creation to Eternal Completion
- the logic of separation, judgment, resurrection, inheritance, and alignment

At the close of Month 4, nothing remains untaught.

From this point forward, the student is no longer evaluated on comprehension.

They are evaluated on transfer.

CLOSING DECLARATION

TERM IV taught the system.

TERM V proves the system has been absorbed.

From here forward:

- Yada Yahuah is no longer received
- It is demonstrated

Instruction has ended.

Alignment is now revealed.

CONCLUSION — BOOK 4 →› BOOK 5

Transition to MBRS Book 5 — Master-Level Thesis

MBRS Book 4 has completed the instructional architecture of the Master of Biblical Restoration Studies. The full map of humanity has been traced from creation to corruption, from mixture to restoration, from calling to transformation, from mercy to judgment, from resurrection to eternal alignment. No unresolved category remains. No unexplained equation stands incomplete. The Restoration Order has been fully disclosed.
At this stage, instruction ends.

The student now possesses the complete Three Humanities™ framework, the governing Humanity Equations, the restored Yada Yahuah methodology, and the full covenantal logic of Scripture from Bereshith to New Creation. The task is no longer to receive structure, but to demonstrate mastery of structure. No further doctrinal scaffolding will be provided.

MBRS Book 5 therefore marks the Thesis Phase — where the student independently applies, defends, and articulates the Restoration System without instructional guidance. What has been taught must now be proven. What has been received must now be demonstrated. What has been learned must now be owned.

Instruction concludes. Demonstration begins.

TERM IV — GLOSSARY

Adversary (śâṭân): A functional role of accusation or opposition, not a proper name

Assigned Judgment: The specific form of consequence determined by Yahuah and applied according to the nature of the transgression and the role of the transgressor.

Babel (System): The cumulative, trans-generational structure of rebellion that survives by transformation rather than by preserving physical empire. In Week 30, Babel is defined as an administered global order—religious, political, and economic—through which covenant betrayal is normalized and enforced.

Bethabara: A geographic designation associated with the Jordan region, traditionally identified as a place of crossing and renewal. In this module, Bethabara is referenced in relation to covenantal transition, priestly activity, and preparation for restoration within the broader biblical narrative and Qumran.

Bloodguilt: Juridical covenant liability accumulated through preserved violence against Yahuah's witnesses. In Week 30, bloodguilt is the consolidated record of persecution found "in Babel," including prophets, saints, and covenant faithful—demonstrating that the system carries responsibility for cumulative covenant bloodshed.

Book of Life: The covenantal record of those who belong to Yahuah through faithfulness, obedience, and allegiance to Yahusha, representing divine acknowledgment rather than arbitrary inclusion.

Calendar Authority: refers to the governance of worship through control of appointed times as established by Yahuah in Scripture. The only legitimate calendar and authority over time is that which originates with Yahuah and is recorded in the Scriptural witness. Humanity does not possess the authority to alter, redefine, or legislate sacred time. Human attempts to modify or replace the Scriptural calendar—whether through tradition, institutional power, or political decree—constitute usurpation, not authorization, and result in distortion of worship rather than legitimate governance.

Constantine: A Roman emperor historically associated with the formal integration of Christianity into the Roman imperial system. In this module, Constantine is referenced as a representative of imperial religious authority, not as a covenant-appointed guardian of Scripture.

Decretive Judgment: judgment established against an enduring corrupt outcome

Final Extermination: Complete removal of corruption at the appointed end

Harvest: The structural moment when coexistence ends and distinction becomes necessary.

Judgment: Divine containment of irreversible corruption through authoritative decree and restraint. Boundary enforcement that ends corruption's access and secures restored order. Boundary enforcement required when corruption becomes total and publicly enthroned. In Week 30, judgment is not divine volatility; it is the necessary covenant act that ends an irreversible system when rebellion reaches full maturation.

Removal: Termination of corruption that cannot inherit covenant purpose.

Termination: The concluded authority of a corrupted order.

Throne (of Babel): The matured form of post-Flood rebellion in which defiance is no longer localized by proximity (tower), but institutionalized through governance, worship, economy, and doctrine. The throne represents centralized authority that rules by regulation and redefinition rather than chaotic violence.

Universal Defiance: The final stage of rebellion in which kings, nations, merchants, and religious structures are unified under Babel's redefinition of worship and authority. Universal defiance is not merely widespread sin, but coordinated covenant opposition through shared system.

Vindication: The act by which Yahuah publicly and covenantal confirms the righteousness of a faithful servant after suffering, demonstrating that obedience—not opposition or suffering—determines legitimacy and authority.

Final Extermination: Complete removal of corruption at the appointed end.

www.ingramcontent.com/pod-product-compliance
Lightning Source LLC
Chambersburg PA
CBHW080608090426

42735CB00017B/3363